T0193840

The Childlike faith that pleases the savior pours forth as Carole recalls the expectation of Jesus being near to her in her bedroom. Her later years will test that faith to see if her savior is as near to her as she once believed. Carole's real life story of Gods faithfulness is an easy read that will often bring a smile, cause a laugh and emotionally move the reader to consider God's faithfulness in their own lives. In holy scripture the proverbs say "A man who has friends must himself be friendly, But there is a friend who sticks closer than a brother". Proverbs 18:24 (NKJV) This proverb is realized in Carole's truly human story of one expectant child relying on her loving, faithful God for a lifetime!

Pastor Joe Monfreda
Calvary Church of San Dimas, CA

Love Them, Encourage Them, Tell Them About Me!

TRANSFORMED

CAROLE KEALY PHILLIPS

WESTBOW
PRESS®
A DIVISION OF THOMAS NELSON
& ZONDERVAN

WestBow Press books may be ordered through booksellers or by contacting:

WestBow Press
A Division of Thomas Nelson & Zondervan
1663 Liberty Drive
Bloomington, IN 47403
www.westbowpress.com
1 (866) 928-1240

ISBN: 978-1-9736-5861-0 (sc)
ISBN: 978-1-9736-5862-7 (hc)
ISBN: 978-1-9736-5860-3 (e)

Library of Congress Control Number: 2019903840

Print information available on the last page.

WestBow Press rev. date: 04/25/2019

Dedicated
with immense love
to my grandchildren.
I trust that each name
– Jude, Reese, Caleb, Kealy, Paige, Titus and Elle –
will forever remain in the Lamb's Book of Life.
(Revelation 3:5)

Contents

Author's Note

THE HOLY SPIRIT never brings attention to Himself. Rather, He points to Jesus. Therefore, please forgive all the I's in this testimony. It is the only way I know how to tell the facts.

Lord, should I write this? I will take a step of faith and begin to write. If You do not want me to continue, please close the words down.

Some may criticize me for writing this testimony. Christian and non-Christian alike might say, "How did she know that was Jesus?" I write of what little I knew then and what I know even more today.

> For we cannot but speak the things which we have seen
> and heard. (Acts 4:20)

> Love them; encourage them; tell them about Me.

1
Chapter

BEGINNINGS

I WAS BORN THE youngest of seven in London England in the early 1950s. My mother later told me that I was her biggest baby, weighing nine and a quarter pounds. The midwife said, "This one will have her way." Apparently, I had lifted my head off the bed.

> But You, O LORD, are a shield for me, my glory and
> the One who lifts my head. (Psalm 3:3)

As I grew, I could see that we were not the normal run-of-the-mill family that you would typically find in South London. We were different in that Dad was Irish and Mum was Italian, and we couldn't hide this fact because both had accents. To top it off, my paternal grandma was American. Somehow, she ended up living in the basement of a house in London's upper-class Kensington neighborhood. "It's the address that counts," she would mutter. From what I saw, she was a rather ornery individual who, back in the old country (Ireland) was proud of being called the "American lady." My eldest brother, Tony, said that when she would take him to the cinema (he was about four years old, just after World War II), she stubbornly sat during the English national anthem and proudly stood for the American. If he didn't stand with her, she would yank him up by his ear and say, "Stand up."

We were a rowdy bunch! Even our dog was well known in the neighborhood for being a nuisance.

Around the corner from our house, located in South London, my mum and dad owned and operated a working-man's café. My dad would serve the tea, gamble on the horses, and dish out money to anyone who asked him for a loan. My mother? She was a rather ladylike, saintly person who would do all the cooking in the back. She always took the back seat. My sister and I would sometimes work in the café or just hang around. I loved talking to all the old men who came in on a regular basis and told their stories. They would p-o-u-r their tea into a saucer to cool it off and then s-l-u-r-p it down like it was medicine to their bones. The café was a warm, friendly place, and looking back, I realize that my mum and dad cared for the unlovely.

We lived in a crowded, two-story brick house, where the door was always open, and everyone was welcome. I believe that God dropped me off in the middle of the life for me. I always was a very friendly, talkative child; if I wasn't talking, I was singing, so I took to this kind of life—one filled with people—with glee. My mother often asked me to stop inviting everyone to the house for a cup of tea. She would say, "Carole, how is it that you love everyone?" I can still hear her words today and can see that trait in me.

Today I have the full Love of Jesus Christ living in me, but there is still some dying of self to be done. Jesus said, "But if you love those who love you, what credit is that to you? For even sinners love those who love them …" (Luke 6:32). So what kind of love is Jesus speaking of? I have learned that this is the supernatural agape love, the unconditional, self-sacrificing love that took Jesus to the cross when, with His dying words, He said, "Father, forgive them, for they do not know what they do" (Luke 23:34). When we can love in return for hatred, betrayal, and murder, this is when we know that we are on the narrow road that leads to life.

> Because narrow is the gate and difficult is the way that leads to life, and there are few who find it. (Matthew 7:14)

At Christmas, our house almost seemed to burst at the seams, as relatives and friends came to visit. Gifts would come through the mail from as far away as Australia, including dried glazed fruit in pretty packages. We knew that Christmas was about baby Jesus coming into the world to bring us very good things, so our family celebrated by drinking and dancing. I remember one Christmastime when I was maybe four or five years old. I sat on my bed and wondered why everyone was going to get a present for Christmas, but nobody was giving one to Jesus. So on Christmas Eve, I left Jesus a present—a chocolate—behind a wooden picture that sat on the mantel in my bedroom. The picture showed Jesus knocking on a door, but the door had no handle; I wondered where that handle was. On Christmas morning I ran to peek behind the picture, but to my surprise, the chocolate was still there. My heart sank as I wondered why Jesus didn't take His chocolate; after all, it was His birthday, wasn't it?

Jesus was always very real to me. Although my parents didn't speak about Jesus in a personal way, they did make sure that we kids went to church. Their religion seemed important to them. My eldest sister, Bruna, took me to church. She was more than fifteen years older than me, and I loved being with her. I remember holding her hand and running (not walking) alongside her as she walked very fast up Clapham High Street. Unbeknownst to me, this high street, in its day, once housed politician, and a leader of the movement to abolish the slave trade, William Wilberforce and evangelist and teacher Oswald Chambers, who taught at the Bible college there at Clapham Common. C. H. Spurgeon's tabernacle was approximately four or five miles away. A very rich Christian heritage surrounded me, yet I grew up hearing nothing about it.

The church we went to was a big church, and I loved it because I knew that it was God's house. I felt at home in God's house.

> I was glad when they said to me, "Let us go to the house
> of the LORD." (Psalm 122:1)

However, we were not encouraged to read the Bible; in fact, in those days the leaders of the church we belonged to discouraged us from reading it, so we never had a Bible in our house. The Bible—God's Word—says, "My people perish for lack of knowledge" (Hosea 4:6). Was I perishing? Maybe—but I had heard and believed that Jesus died on the cross for my sins. I was so thankful that He did that for me, and I remember thanking Him a lot. I had an overwhelming gratitude for what He did for me.

> Who being the brightness of His glory, and the express image of His person, and upholding all things by the word of His power, when He had by Himself purged our sins, sat down at the right Hand of the Majesty on high. (Hebrews 1:3)

Did my young heart understand fully what this meant? I don't think so, but He was Jesus, and somehow I knew Him.

> The Spirit Himself bears witness with our spirit that we are children of God, and if children, then heirs—heirs of God and joint heirs of Christ. (Romans 8:16–17)

My daddy was a very significant part of my early life, as it was with all little girls. I loved him so much, although deep down inside, I was sad because he drank a lot. I would hear the men in the café mocking him. I felt sorry for him. My friends thought that he was my grandad, as he was fifty years old when I was born. But I truly loved him. On that evening when he fell and cut his eyebrow, it seemed as if I had something to tell him, but all I could do was watch the blood slowly trickle down his face. He'd fallen because he was too drunk to stand. By his side, trying to prop him up, was an Irish cousin of ours, Dermot, who actually worked for Scotland Yard as a young detective. I looked at my dad, and he looked back at me, and his eyes filled with tears as he said, "Baba, don't look at me like that." I didn't know how I was looking at him, but I knew that

I loved him with a deep supernatural, protective kind of love. Did this love come from the Holy Spirit?

Some nights I would lie in bed and say to Jesus, "Heaven must be lovely because everyone there loves one another!" I knew that Jesus was in my room with me.

> But there is a spirit in a man, and the breath of the Almighty gives him understanding. (Job 32:8)

It was as though He was erasing all of the data from my mind by touching my forehead, and as if He was saying, "Be strong and of good courage," and "I will never leave you nor forsake you." I felt safe. Nestled together in this time of visitation, I saw two visions that I can still see today, exactly as I saw them then.

> In a dream, in a vision of the night, when deep sleep falls upon men, while slumbering on their beds, then He opens the ears of men, and seals their instruction in order to turn man from his deed, and conceal pride from man. He keeps back his soul from the Pit and his life from perishing … (Job 33:15-18)

The first was an image of an older, gray-haired lady, who was dressed in a khaki safari uniform as if in Africa, with her hair tucked into her circular safari hat. Her form seemed fit and slender. She looked straight at me as she was half bent over, working. I could not see her face but knew she was eighty-one years old. At the time I didn't think much of it, only that I knew she was in Africa, and she looked like my paternal grandma. I suppose my grandma was the only really old person I knew at the time. All of it seemed so normal.

The other image I saw was of me, as if I was at the back of a stage, looking at the back of myself. I was dressed in a school uniform, and my brown hair was neatly cut into a bob. I may have been about twelve years old. In the vision, I saw myself standing on a stage or at a podium, and many people were looking back at me. I probably was speaking to them, but what was I telling them? All I know is that the visions seemed normal to me, and I didn't question them at all.

> For the vision is yet for an appointed time; But at the end
> it will speak, and it will not lie, though it tarries, wait for
> it; Because it will surely come … (Habakkuk 2:3)

I felt so close to Jesus, and I wanted to be with Him where He was, but I knew I had to walk this journey ahead of me, and I knew He wanted me to. I told my family about the lady in Africa, but I don't think anyone heard.

By the time I was five years old, I had learned that I had a sister in Italy. Christine was two years my senior. Before I was born, she was sent to Italy to my mum's family. In the cold London air, Christine had contracted whooping cough, and my mum and dad decided that the Italian air would do her good. I believe the plan was to bring her home when she was better, but with six other children and a busy work life, months turned into years. Christine finally came home to England when she was seven years old. My dad told me one day that Christine was finally coming home and that we would be driving to the train station to pick her up.

He had two dolls in his arms and said to me, "Baba, which doll shall we give Christine?" In my heart, I knew that he wanted me to give up the bigger doll, and I did with full surrender. I truly wanted Christine to have the bigger doll, and she loved it. My dad loaded up the Rolls-Royce (my dad was a car buff and a lovable showoff), and it seemed I was the only one in the back seat. I cannot remember if my mother was sitting up front with my dad, but nevertheless, we were off to meet my sister, Christine, and bring her home.

The next memory I have is of me sitting in the back seat of the Rolls-Royce with Christine. She tells me that I slipped my hand into hers; I can't remember, but I know that I loved her and was glad she was home. It must have been extremely hard for her, as she had no understanding of the English language. After all, her language for the past seven years had been Italian, and that was all she knew. She must have felt very confused, as she was taken from the only home she had ever known and was suddenly faced with six rowdy siblings that she had never met before and couldn't understand. Her uncle and aunt, whom she knew as her mother and father, were now gone, and she had a new set of parents (that is a story for her to tell).

Later, she told me that she thought of me as an angel in the back seat of the car, but alas, it was only me. Was there something I had to tell her? Maybe I would tell her later. Although I'd never seen her, I knew her. We became close friends and remain so to this day.

Three sisters and I shared a bedroom. Our two older sisters, Sandra (whom I called Nan Nan) and Barbara, had a single bed each in opposite sides of the room. Christine and I shared a double bed that faced the two big windows that looked onto the wonderful sight of Big Ben Scaffolding, an industrial scaffolding welding factory. Each morning we awoke to the high-pitched, piercing sound of sparks flying off steel poles as they were being welded and the tinny, accompanying sound of hollow poles hitting the ground. This was my home, and I was a happy. Christine and I had many friends in the neighborhood. Wherever we were, they wanted to be (maybe because there were two of us). We were always on a mission.

Our summer holidays consisted of getting up late and walking up to Clapham Common with a group of kids from the neighborhood to climb trees, fish at the pond, and look for animals. I was in love with animals. I had cats, dogs, guinea pigs, hamsters, birds, and tortoises. My dad would say to me, "Baba, what do you want next in the backyard, an elephant?"

During the long summer evenings, we would play outdoors until nine o'clock or later. England has a long twilight period in the summer, and it doesn't really get dark till after ten o'clock. On a number of those summer days, we would get caught in short showers of rain. I remember the smell of the brick walls after the rain had washed them clean—almost edible to me. Life was easy and free. I loved my at-home childhood.

School was a different story. I wasn't the same at school as I was at home, and I felt it deeply. I remember lying in bed at night and asking Jesus to make me the same at school as I was at home. I liked who I was at home, but at school I was so shy. At home I was funny and free and loved being that way, but at school I was very intimidated, and I was too shy to speak up in class or with my classmates. I was horrified when, at the age of around nine, I was asked by my teacher to stand up in class and read a story I had written. The story was about Paddington Bear, and I had written it with a funny twist. I stood up (knowing there was no way out), and once I muttered the first word, I then managed to stumble through it. The teacher may as well have asked me to jump off a cliff, and with a choice, I would have gladly jumped.

I remember my first day of school. I was five years old. In my mind's eye, I still see a small wooden desk next to another small desk and opposite two others—the desks were in groups of four. Opposite me sat my new friend Vivien Bunn. She seemed a little scared but not quite like me, or so it seemed. I was terrified to be away from my home where I felt happy and secure. As I watched my mother leave, and slowly walk away, I put my forehead on the desk and quietly cried. It seemed that I should be at home for my mum. She would miss our time at breakfast when I would sit on her lap, and we would eat toast and orange-peel marmalade together. There must have been something I needed to tell her. Maybe I would tell her later. Orange was my favorite color because it was the color of times when I was closest to my mum. I suppose Vivien became my first best friend at school.

By the mid-1950s in England, we began to see an influx of people coming into the country from Pakistan, India, and parts of Africa. "Why not?" said my mother. "England has had her fingers in every pie."

A lovely girl from Pakistan was in my class at school. Her name was Valerie. She had lovely long black hair, and we became friends quite quickly. One day Valerie wasn't at school. I never saw her again. A week or so passed, and one day I arrived home from school to find my mum reading the newspaper. She asked me if I had a friend called Valerie at school. The newspaper article read, "Father sets light to daughter's buttocks in garage." This was the first I had ever heard of what is known as an "honor killing." An honor killing happens in certain cultures. It is the killing of a relative, especially a girl or woman, who is perceived to have brought dishonor to the family. Valerie was gone, and what was it that I should have told her? I felt certain that she needed to know, but what was it?

I had quite a few friends at school, but I always managed to have just one best friend. It always seemed that others wanted to sit next to me, especially my neighborhood friends. They usually would say, "I begsy sitting next to Carole." We would use this term *begsy* when we were vying for something. I always wondered why they wanted to sit by me. My mother later told me that people who knew me wanted to own me. That is how it felt. But it wasn't always so sweet.

When I was about eight years old, there was a conflict between another girl in my class and me. I was standing in the school playground at the head of a single line of other children. Opposite me was Denise, an aggressive born leader, with a line of kids behind her; it was as if I had my army, and she had hers. The conflict was over a broken Christmas present that she had given me. I wasn't bothered about the present being broken, but she said that I'd broke it purposely. That wasn't true. Even then, I hated deceit. Was there something I should have told her?

On another occasion, I was standing in the lunch line, and David told me to move back, as I was in the wrong place. I would not, and he started hitting me. We scrambled to the floor, and I pulled his ear. He told me to stop pulling his ear, and when I wouldn't, he hit me on the nose. My eyes went black—he had broken my nose. Was God preparing me for the real battles of life? Maybe He was getting me ready for the divisions that would come when I finally did tell them what He wants me to tell them, but what was it?

Time drifted on, and I looked forward to my free and easy weekends. By the time my sister Christine was twelve and I ten, we would take a London double-decker bus to London's National and Tate Galleries. We ate our lunch gazing at Van Gogh and Turner, Raphael and Goya. This eventually would inspire me to go to art school. Outside of the National Gallery was Trafalgar Square, a wonderful place to hang around and sit on the historic statues while feeding the pigeons. For a few pence, we would buy a bag of bird food and see how many pigeons would land on our heads and hands as we stood there. Their scrawny little feet felt strange on my hands and head. I loved every minute of it.

But where was Jesus? Had I forgotten Him? Oh no, He was always there when I needed Him. I knew He loved me; after all, I was a pretty good kid. I didn't want to hurt anyone, and I said my prayers. By the way, everyone sins, and Jesus died on the cross to forgive all of us, right? We still went to church; it was something Christine and I both did. But remember, I only had a prayer book—no Bible—and so I had no knowledge of what Jesus said. Will You teach me, Lord?

> Teach me what I do not see; If I have done iniquity, I will do no more? (Job 34:32)

How could I know Him if I didn't know what He said? Would I refrain from going against His will if I knew His Word?

> Your Word have I hidden in my heart that I may not sin against You. (Psalm 119:25)

By the time I was fourteen, my dad was having tests at the hospital and eventually needed surgery. When they opened him up, they found cancer. They tried to remove the cancer from his lungs, but I heard it was malignant, and as they went in to constrict it, it spread. They sewed him up and sent him home; there was nothing they could do. He had a large gash across his back, and sometimes it would fester. I'll never forget my mother coming home from the hospital after his operation. She had a peakèd look on her face, and she told us my dad had lung cancer and cirrhosis of the liver, and he was given a year to live. The pain I felt was unbearable. It seemed that no one was discussing anything, maybe because nobody knew what to do or say.

What do you say to or about someone who is dying? I think there was definitely something I needed to tell my dad, but I was not sure what. I didn't know what to do with the pain, so I stuffed it and put on a brave face. My dad didn't know that he was going to die soon, and no one told him. In those days, they told the next of kin (my mother). I suppose they thought that if people know they have cancer, they give up and die. So we hid it. As he grew worse, he became bedridden, and I would sit with him. I would clean his wound and rebandage it.

His sister came to see him once but never came back. Maybe she just couldn't handle death. Perhaps there was something I could have told her to give her hope, but I wasn't quite sure what is was. Toward the end, my dad would relive his life. It was as though he was watching an old movie reel, rolling backward. My mother recalled the names from his past.

One day the doctor came and gave my mother a prescription for some medicine to ease his pain. My mother gave it to me, but my sister Sandra, who was twenty-three years old at the time, left work to meet me at the chemist. After a while, the pharmacist, a nice gentleman, came out and said to us, "Who is this for?" We told him it was for our dad, to which he replied, "Is your father very ill?" We said yes, and we walked home with the prescription filled. I found out that the medicine was morphine, which was to "ease him over." Sometimes my dad would throw off his blankets and try to get out of bed, as if to run away. He seemed frightened.

My sister-in-law Margaret would come to eat lunch with my mum and me, and one day we were in my dad's room, and he said, "Take my hand." All three of us took his hand, and he said, "I am going to a new world now." What new world was he speaking of?

By faith we understand that the worlds were framed by
the word of God, so that the things which are seen were
not made of things which are visible. (Hebrews 11:3)

Had my dad been given some knowledge of this new world? I had
asked my mother for his ring, and the day I asked for it, the ring fell off
his finger. I cannot remember how long after that he went to that new
world—maybe a few days or so—but I think I had something to tell him
before he left. But it was too late. At ten minutes before five o'clock on
that cold February morning, I heard a loud wail, which startled me. I
realized it was the wail of death, a sound that comes from the innermost
part of a person's being. The wail came from deep within my mother's
soul. My dad had gone to that new world. It took some time until they
allowed me to go in and see him. He was cold, and as I kissed his
forehead, I thought of those hard brick walls after the summer shower
that used to smell so good. This smell of death didn't smell so good. It
was like kissing hard, cold stone. I walked away.

The trauma was so strong that, physically, I was broken. My system
was not working properly, and I had to go into hospital for a short
procedure at a later time. It seemed that nothing would ever be the
same. My innocent and rather naive life became very hypocritical and
maybe even cynical. I wore a mask that was supposed to tell the world
that I was just fine. Outside of the home, I laughed when I wanted to
cry. I did a pretty good job pretending that I was happy and became the
class clown, which helped me forget the sadness. Each morning I would
do something funny to make the class laugh; it was working. I was a
happy clown, and they were out of control, laughing. But no one knew
the depths of my sorrow inside.

I remembered back to when my dad was still here. I had come
home from school after four of us girls had been in a talent show. It was
1965, and we performed a Beatles song; we were John, Paul, George,
and Ringo. To our surprise, when we finished playing the song and lip
syncing to it, the whole school went into an uproar. This was the time of
Beatlemania, and every girl in the audience ran toward us. The teachers

could do nothing. All the third- and fourth-level girls were screaming and chasing us. Eventually, the crowds dispersed, and we all went home.

My dad (now too ill to work in the café) answered the door and said with a grin, "What happened to you?" The sleeves on my school uniform cardigan were ripped from the shoulders. When I told him what had happened, he laughed. This was the first time in my life that I saw my mum and dad together, and they were home when I got home from school, living a normal life. I think their love for one another was being restored. I was fifteen when my dad died, and because I didn't know what Jesus had said in His Word, I had no promises to hold on to; I had no manual to live by.

Instead, I blamed God for all of my misery. I was very angry at God. I began to build a brick wall around my heart. No one was allowed to get close. Those wonderful childhood years when we used to laugh and play were gone. I missed my dad. How could God have taken him from me? I hadn't had time to sit with him and talk about things. Why, God? Why? I thought back to that picture in my bedroom, the one with Jesus knocking on the door. Maybe that door had no handle so it could keep everyone out. Maybe I wanted that door to be kept shut.

2
Chapter

SEARCHING

I WAS SEARCHING FOR something that had some meaning or maybe just trying to escape from the pain.

> Search me, O God, and know my heart; try me, and know my anxieties; (Psalm 139:23)

I did what I did best, and that was to go! So shortly after my dad died, I talked my sister and two friends into leaving home for some sun. We were going to work at a summer camp in Torquay. Torquay is located on the Devon coast in the south of England. We left on April 27, leaving my mother, one of my sisters, and my brother at home—they were company enough for her. We had signed up to get the camp ready for opening day at the end of May. Little did we know that at this time of year, it was absolutely freezing by the sea. London was much milder.

We met a wonderful couple who worked at the camp, Ralph and Cosy. They were our age, and Cosy was a professing Christian, something I had never really come across before. The few who went to church in my neighborhood belonged to our church. In England, it seemed that our Protestant friends never had to go to church at all. Cosy seemed different, and she would get very upset with us when we would discuss astrology (I was learning how to do astrological charts) and play around with the Ouija board. To us it was just intriguing fun, but to her, I learned later, it was idolatry.

> But where are your gods you made for yourselves? Let them arise, if they can save you when you are in trouble; (Jeremiah 2:28)

Did she have something to tell us about false gods? She probably tried, but at this time in my life, I was searching for an identity. Could I have been opening a door for the enemy of our souls to take a foothold in my life? Was astrology a false god? Of course I knew about Jesus, but I didn't know if I could find my identity in Him. I just wasn't thinking about Him much, unless, of course, I needed Him.

> And you will seek Me and find Me, when you search for Me with all of your heart. I will be found by you, says the LORD, and I will bring you back from your captivity; (Jeremiah 29:13–14)

Astrology, palm reading, and psychics were much more exciting, and I thought they might show me why I was here and who I was. So I dabbled.

> You are wearied in the multitude of your counsels; Let now the astrologers, the stargazers, and the monthly prognosticators stand up and save you … (Isaiah 47:13)

I hadn't really thought about being saved. The job at the camp entailed cleaning everything in sight. We had to be ready for opening day. One cold, windy day, we were cleaning the snack bar/kiosk that was located on the beach. There I met John, a short, fair-haired boy who seemed to be a deep thinker; he was a little older than me. We would talk for hours about the afterlife and spiritual matters, but I don't remember Jesus's name coming up. I told John about the lady I used to see and that she was behind the brick wall at the end of our back garden. I could only see the top half of her; she was dressed in a gray cardigan and looked like a schoolteacher. She would whisper to me, but I never knew what she was saying. I told John that I didn't like her but that recently she seemed to be gone.

> And when they say to you, "Seek those who are mediums and wizards, who whisper and mutter," should not a people seek their God? Should they seek the dead on behalf of the living? (Isaiah 8:19)

He asked me if someone close to me had died. I told him my dad, and he said no more. John was there and then gone; I never saw him again. At camp the hours were long and hard. We scrubbed floors, ovens, pots, pans, and the like, but we were a little too immature to keep to this commitment. We thought about leaving, but where would we live? This job came with room and board. But there was a better place—a renowned artist colony in Cornwall called Saint Ives, and as the wannabe hippie that I was, I had the brilliant idea for us four girls to move there. It wasn't too far away. So I convinced all three girls to chance it. If it didn't work out, we would go home.

On a very cold day in late May, we hitchhiked and arrived at this wonderful, quaint town of Saint Ives and began looking for jobs. We started with the newspaper. Then I suggested that we go to church and ask Jesus for help. I knew that if anyone could help, it would be Jesus. So in the middle of the afternoon (on my birthday), all four of us went to church. I knelt down and prayed, believing that Jesus would help us—and He did.

> Likewise the Spirit also helps us in our weaknesses. For we do not know what we should pray for as we ought, but the Spirit Himself makes intercession for us, with groanings that cannot be uttered. (Romans 8:26)

The next day we got two job offers. My friend and I went to one house to clean and look after Jonathan, a naughty three-year-old; and my sister and her friend went to another house to work. We rented a mobile trailer to live in, which was in the middle of a field, where cows quietly grazed. One weekend I was outside, painting a landscape. Music played rather loudly from inside our trailer. We noticed that some cows had gathered around us and eventually surrounded our caravan. I quickly picked up my art supplies and ran inside, shutting the door just before the cows began to gore our trailer. They barged into it, causing it to rock back and forth. Cups flew, things fell, and as for us, we were quite scared! We turned the music off, and after a few moos, they walked away. They got their point across; they didn't like Bob Dylan's voice as much as we did.

Although this was fun and new, the novelty soon wore off, and the loss of my dad weighed heavily on me. I don't know how his death affected my sister. I think that my own grief prevented me from seeing beyond that. I cried and acted out around my sister and friends. They were kind and understanding. In fact, my friend Sandra had lost her mother when she was only eleven years old. How could I be so selfish? I wallowed in my grief over the death of my dad. I knew that if he had been here, I would have laughed with him and danced with him and told him what I needed to tell him—but what was it that I had to tell him? I knew it was something of the utmost importance—but what?

At the end of June we all went back home to London. I was sixteen, and at the age of sixteen I fell in love. I noticed a young boy at the bus stop in my neighborhood whom I'd never seen before. We chatted about music and such, and on another occasion, I happened to see him walking down my street. I saw the house that he went into, and I wondered how I could get to talk to him again. Always very resourceful, I arranged with one of my friends to pretend that I was doing a survey for the college I attended. I could then go to his house to ask questions. I made up some questions and went with my friend to knock on his door.

A tall, blonde lady answered, and I told her that we were looking to ask some questions of the young people of the house that related to our age group.

"Oh yes," she said with a smile and called, "Michael!"

So that's his name, I thought.

And he came out to talk to us. Somehow, I managed to ask the questions and got his opinion on the issues of the day. From that time on, we would stop to talk when we saw one another. We both loved Bob Dylan's deep, poetic music; in fact, Micky (as we called him) played the guitar. I was so in love. But he had a sad past and was mourning his own losses. I found it very hard to let him know just how much I cared about him. Yet over the years, we saw each other often. He came to my sister Christine's twenty-first birthday party. We danced together, and then, out of the blue, he began to talk about heaven. He said he could see himself with his guitar and me with my paintbrushes. This would have been the perfect time to tell him what I had to tell him, but I didn't know what it was. So again we parted ways, and very soon afterward, I began to date someone else.

In 1969 I turned eighteen, and our family moved from our old two-story brick house to a brand-new flat in Tulse Hill, which had a few small flats nestled in between some nice older homes. My mother was quite happy with something new and clean. The odd part is that Micky had lived in this area and was back here. I was now in his neck of the woods. We were always bumping into one another. *Maybe I should tell him what I am supposed to tell him,* I thought.

Unfortunately, that day never came. I lost the opportunity. I will never forget the day when I arrived home from college, and my mother looked at me rather strangely. Then, after hesitating, she said a girl who she thought might be Micky's girlfriend had come by to see me. The girl had left her phone number but she'd said that Micky had died. He had drowned in the bath. Apparently, the pilot light on the water heater had gone out; carbon monoxide was the silent killer. I went numb and asked no questions.

> For there is not a word on my tongue, but behold O
> Lord, You know it altogether ... (Psalm 139:4)

There were no words to speak. What words speak of death? I didn't go to his funeral. His mother, to whom I had grown quite close, must have been devastated. He died in that old house she still lived in, the one where we would often talk.

Now, tell me, Lord, was there something that I should have told Micky? And what about his mother? Will You tell him what I didn't tell him?

I went back to college to gain some credits. My aim was art school, but without passing certain exams, it was hard to get in. By 1970, at the age of nineteen, I finally was accepted. That was also the year that my sister, Christine, and I went to the now-famous Isle of Wight festival, along with over six hundred thousand other fans—it was the English equivalent of Woodstock. The only reason I wanted to go was because Bob Dylan was to perform, along with Jimmy Hendrix and other famous rock stars of the day. Was this the identity I was looking for? Art school, along with listening to the depth of Bob Dylan's words, just seemed to work for me. I could draw pretty well, and my teacher (a local renowned artist himself) told me that I was one of the better drawers in the class, but he added, "If only you had the discipline to stay with it."

Alas, *staying with it* was just not in my vocabulary. I left after a year or so but continued to paint at home. My mother displayed one of my larger paintings, which portrayed ancient, Semitic-looking men and women, some pointing up and some looking up; the expressions on their faces showed fear and doom.

> They will pass through it hard pressed and hungry, that
> they will be enraged and curse their king and their God,
> and look upward. Then they will look to the earth and
> see trouble, even darkness, gloom of anguish; and they
> will be driven into darkness. (Isaiah 8:21–22)

When the priest from our church came to visit my mum, he pointed at the painting and said, "This is very biblical, It looks like the children of Israel in the wilderness." When my mother told me what he had said, I wondered if Jesus was speaking to me. These were the idolatrous and apostate Israelites who were distracted, not knowing where to go, or what to do; whereas if they had not forsaken God, they might have a quiet and settled abode in the land. Was the Lord showing me my sin through my painting? I couldn't have been pleasing Him by living life my way. I was still looking for something, but what was it?

I left art school realizing that it was not possible for me to paint pretty pictures for my entire life. I had to earn my keep. So I looked for a job at one of the bigger employment agencies in London. The lady interviewing me asked if I would consider working in the employment industry. She said that she thought that I was "cheeky enough." I agreed to go for personality testing and got the job. I was hired to place local people in local jobs.

The agency was large, which made it possible for me to work on a local basis, as there were enough offices to choose from. I was in a startup office and did exceedingly well. I became quite the success at placing administrative people in suitable job openings in the area. People came in and asked to see *only* me. Aunts, brothers, or sisters of someone I'd placed came lining up to see me. You might imagine what this did to my popularity among my coworkers—those young girls did not like this at all. One of them was very aggressive and would scream at me and embarrass me in front of the people waiting to see me. It was an unusual situation in the natural world. Something supernatural was taking place. Maybe it was a gift that God gave me to draw people to Him and minister to them—and to tell them what I was supposed to tell them. If only I knew what that was. I didn't understand much, yet I knew that this was not my doing. In my mind's eye, I saw myself putting my head on my desk and saying, "This is not me; this has to be God."

But there is a spirit in man, And the breath of the Almighty gives him understanding. (Job 32:8)

I am the vine, you are the branches, he who abides in Me, and I in him, bears much fruit, for without Me you can do nothing. (John 15:5)

I became known as the Millionaire Interviewer, and managers used my name to dangle the carrot in front of young beginners to motivate them to make more money. I was beginning to earn a very good wage, but I wasn't motivated by money—and I wasn't staying too long either. I needed to go! I wanted to travel, and I knew that I always had a job to come back to on my return to London. Over the next three years or so, I worked for two of the major agencies in London, and when I left, I was assured of a job when I returned, but I never did return to stay.

Funny how things turn out because around this time I finally made contact with Micky's girlfriend and brought her into our group of friends. She was depressed over Micky's death and asked if I would be interested in traveling somewhere for a few months. She asked the right person; I was ready to go. She wanted to go to Australia, but I wanted to go to America. She responded to my suggestion with a resounding *no*. But she had a cousin in Canada who would let us stay with her, so we settled for Canada.

It was June 1974, and I had just turned twenty-three. My friend and I would be flying out of London's Heathrow airport to Toronto, Canada. My brother Jimmy volunteered to take us to the airport, and my mother came along. During the drive, I asked Jimmy if he would like to join us in Canada at some point. It seemed to me that something wasn't quite right between him and his wife. She was going back to the north of England, where she was from. He told me that he was considering going to Spain with a mutual friend of ours. Jimmy was five years older than me, so we weren't extremely close, but we shared a love for Bob Dylan's music, and we had spent some time seeking spiritual things together.

He once took me to a Hindu religious meeting; we both were seeking in a spiritual sense.

We said our farewells at the airport, but I went back to give him another hug. Why was that? There must have been something that I needed to tell him.

3

Chapter

CROSSING OVER

THIS WAS THE first time that I crossed the Atlantic but definitely was not to be the last. Upon arriving in Canada, Irene (my friend) and I settled in with our new family—Irene's cousin, Jeanette, her husband, and two lovely children. Their home was our base while away from home. We began our journey from Toronto and headed west, seeing many beautiful sites. We bought a one-way train ticket to Vancouver, a three-day journey from Toronto. I will never forget waking up and looking out of the window as we passed through the majestic Canadian Rockies. We saw beautiful Banff and Lake Louise. I had seen Switzerland, but this seemed even more monumental. In the ensuing days, there was much adventure and many stories to tell; none of them, however, has much meaning today, as I found something far more beautiful.

By August we were back in Toronto and headed east to Nova Scotia and Newfoundland. I didn't know it, but at this particular time, my family had been trying to contact me, all in vain. Unaware that I needed to know about something back home, we traveled on to Prince Edward Island. We stayed in many youth hostels, but one in particular stuck in my mind. As I was lying in bed, just before dozing off, I saw a vivid figure outside the window.

I asked Irene, "Can you see that?"

I thought she said yes, but nothing else was said.

The figure I saw looked like a waiter. He had a white napkin-type cloth thrown over his arm, as if he was serving something. He wore a goatee, and there was a darkness about him. His silhouette was turned to the side. He seemed very real. Did he have something to tell us?

We continued on our journey, and by the end of August, we were in Prince Edward Island. We found the open-air youth hostel where we would stay for the next couple of nights and pitched our tent. We always met many fellow travelers, and I had been talking to a young boy from London—it was always good to meet someone from our home city. This was a good time to get a cigarette and enjoy the company. I went into the tent to get my cigarettes, and as I was backing out, I heard a voice (Canadian or American) ask, "Do you need a light?" I stood up to see an attractive young guy, his face buried in his coarse dark hair. His dark moustache accentuated his kind light-colored eyes. His name was Terry, and he and his friend had driven up on their motorcycles from America to travel the eastern part of Canada. They were heading to Labrador.

My friend and I jumped on the back of their motorcycles, and we went downtown to eat. Late August in Canada can be quite cold, and my hands were freezing on the back of that motorcycle. Terry gave me his gloves. *How very kind*, I thought. I felt safe with him.

Later, back at the camp, we played cards and hung around until late. The next morning before they left, Terry gave me his phone number. I kept it but didn't think there was much use in calling him. After all, he was going to Labrador and wouldn't be at that number for weeks. We said our farewells, and within days, my friend and I started back west to Toronto.

When we arrived at our base in early September, a telegram from London was awaiting me. I knew it wasn't good, but my friend said, "Oh, you know your mum. She's probably just worried about you."

No, I knew it wasn't good. I called my mother, and on the other end of the phone, her monotone voice quietly said, "Carole, Jimmy is dead."

Thoughts of my brother flooded my mind. Had I heard her correctly? I wanted to backtrack and change what she had just said.

I braced myself and asked, "Was it cancer? Was it an accident? What was it?"

"He killed himself," she said.

My mind drifted back to the picture on my mantel. It made no sense to me that Jesus was even knocking on that door. Surely He didn't want to open it, not now. Where was God in all of this? Couldn't He have stopped Jimmy from doing this? I was completely numb, the numbness that death brings—shock. What had happened to Jimmy? Why would he do such a thing when he had so much to live for?

> There is a way that seems right to a man, but its end is the way of death. (Proverbs 14:12)

What would happen to his wife? My mother went on to explain that Jimmy had learned that his wife had left him and was living back up north. My mind wandered. *Oh, so that was it. I suppose that he could not stand the thought of her leaving him, and because he was in so much pain, he tried to kill the pain but killed himself instead.*

My mother later explained that Jimmy had been staying at his mother-in-law's house and found some pills in her cabinet. When the coroner arrived, Jimmy was found with his fingers in his mouth, as if trying to bring the pills back. He'd had second thoughts but too late. My elder brother, Tony, took care of all the details. The coroner's office gave him a letter that Jimmy had written. At the end of the letter, Jimmy wrote, "Open your arms up, sweet Jesus, and take me in."

My thoughts scrambled back to the last time I'd seen Jimmy at the airport. I had gone back a second time to say farewell. But I didn't think that it was goodbye forever. I am sure that there was something that I needed to tell him before he left.

At the end of the phone call, my mother said they'd tried to contact me via radio and other media to no avail. She then said, "Carole, don't come home right now. It is all over."

When I put the phone down, I wanted to be alone. I began to drink as much wine as I could to try to drown the pain. I didn't want to talk to anyone. At the young age of twenty-three, I had experienced the cold shudder of death three times. Three people that I truly loved and would never see again.

My friend didn't know what to do for me. She had met someone she liked, so she probably thought it would be good for me to have someone to be with. She said, "Call that boy you met on Prince Edward Island."

"No, he won't be home for weeks," I said.

But she somehow managed to get Terry's phone number and called it. Surprisingly, he was there and told my friend that he would come up to Canada to meet me. When God has a plan, He doesn't have to move mountains to make it come to pass. He breaks motorcycles.

Apparently, Terry's motorcycle had started leaking, and he didn't want to chance going all the way to Labrador, so he went to his parents' house in Pennsylvania. I was relieved. In a way, I wanted to be with someone I could trust. Did God bring Terry? God was really working because why would Terry, someone who didn't even know me, offer to meet with me?

I'm also still in awe that my friend and I got a visa to enter the United States for ten days. We got it somehow when we were in Vancouver; it was a God thing. It definitely was not the norm because at the American Embassy we were told that we were young and employable. This meant that if we were to come into the United States and try to work it would be construed as taking a job away from an American citizen. The government made it quite clear to us that for this reason it was not possible for us to enter the United States.

I was to meet Terry at the Greyhound bus station in Niagara Falls at the Canadian border. I don't remember saying farewell to my friend or boarding the Greyhound bus. The weight of Jimmy's sudden death lay heavy on my shoulders, almost like a yoke used to join animals together to plow a field. Only I wasn't sharing the weight of the yoke; I was carrying it alone.

> Come to Me, all you who labor and are heavy laden,
> and I will give you rest. Take My yoke upon you and
> learn from Me, for I am gentle and lowly in heart, and
> you will find rest for your souls. For My yoke is easy and
> My burden is light. (Matthew 11:28–30)

I had no rest in my soul, and I didn't want to talk about it or tell anyone what Jimmy had done. Rather, I would live a lie and put on a happy face. My thoughts were scattered. What would God say about what Jimmy had done? Wasn't suicide murder, a crime against God? I was reminded of when my dad died, and then Micky, and how I pretended to be okay when dealing with people I didn't know. If I could just hide my feelings, I would make it through. But my friend told Terry about Jimmy and what he had done, so he already knew. Oh, why wasn't I just going home? There were no answers, and it was as if I was being guided in a supernatural way. I had no direction. I seemed to just float along with no understanding of where I was going or why.

Oh, dear Jesus, what happened? Is Jimmy with You? Jesus did You open up Your arms and receive Jimmy, like he asked? Is Jimmy with You now? So many questions. Will You answer me, Jesus? Will You?

> It shall come to pass that before they call, I will answer;
> and while they are still speaking, I will hear. (Isaiah
> 65:24)

I thought back to the conversation on the phone with my mother; she'd said she'd been trying to contact me. I thought of the image in that youth hostel. Who was that image? A sinister waiter with a goatee? Was that the bringer of bad news, the Grim Reaper?

> So the great dragon was cast out, that serpent of old,
> called the Devil and Satan who deceives the whole
> world. (Revelation 12:9)

The jolt of the bus coming to a halt shook me, distracting my thoughts. We had arrived in Niagara. I remembered nothing of the cities we passed through or the sights that I might have seen. I was completely immersed in my thoughts.

I noticed Terry as soon as I got off the bus. As I spotted him, I felt a pang of embarrassment. Why was I here? I didn't want to lay my burden on Terry. I decided not to; instead, I'd put on my brave face. Terry had borrowed his dad's car. *How nice of his parents to do that.* They probably wondered what kind of person was coming. After all, I was a young girl, and their son was a young man and we were traveling together, alone. This was not how I had been taught to do things. I was not the person I was portraying myself to be. I didn't search too deeply within; it was much too hard to look in there. I lived on the surface. Above my true feelings, which had been stuffed down since my father's demise. Then who was I?

I think I was a long way from that little girl back in Clapham who loved everyone. Maybe, deep down, she was still there, but so many people had died since then. If I'd had the courage to be truthful with myself, I would have realized that I was a fornicator, among other things.

Do you not know that the unrighteous will not inherit the kingdom of God? Do not be deceived. Neither fornicators, nor idolaters, nor adulterers, nor homosexuals, nor sodomites, nor thieves, nor covetous, nor drunkards, nor revilers, nor extortioners will inherit the kingdom of God. (1 Corinthians 6:9-10)

Terry and I drove across the border into America and headed south to his parents' home in the Poconos. In September or October in the Poconos, God puts on the greatest display of color this side of heaven. It was one of the most beautiful sights I had ever seen. Those enormous trees were dressed up in yellow-golden frills. As each leaf danced in the breeze, the sunlight illuminated them, and they twinkled like stars as they twirled in the wind. The afternoon sun sparked the orange and red leaves, setting them ablaze like a fiery furnace.

Terry didn't ask too many questions or say too much. I had a feeling that he knew what pain felt like. Later, I learned that he had gone through a similar ordeal with his girlfriend as my brother had experienced. In the ensuing days, the long drives he took me on were medicine for my soul. I thought of Jimmy and my poor mother and wished that I could share some of the tranquility with them. Maybe we would, one day in heaven. Terry took me to all his favorite hangouts—the local pubs and diners. I loved being with him. The days went quickly, and soon it was late September. Within days of arriving, I felt the cool air approaching. The sun was getting weaker, and I was running out of time. My visa would soon expire. I must go!

Oh, how I always loved to hear that word *go*! But this time I would have preferred to hear *stay*. That was not possible. After saying my farewells to Terry's parents, who had been so good to me (they were Christians), Terry and I drove back to my base in Canada.

Was there something (besides thank you) that I needed to tell Terry before I left him? I wasn't sure. But I did tell him that I was very thankful for all he had given me. There was so much more that I wanted to say to him, but, as the song goes, my words got in the way. So I did what I did best; I left.

I arrived in London in late September. I remembered nothing of how I got from the airport to home. I don't remember seeing my mother's face. I just know that she was never the same. Her eyes were always red and sore, as if she was crying continually. My being back with her, I think, helped her a little. She said when I came home, it was like a breath of fresh air for her. I later learned that God's *ruach* (Hebrew) is the source of life. It is the breath of God, and means wind or spirit in the Hebrew. *Ruach Elohim* is used in Genesis 1:2, where it speaks of the Spirit hovering over the face of the waters.

I would have loved to have been a breath of fresh air for my dear mother. Maybe I was for the first week or so, but when I got bored and life showed no exciting results, I became moody and miserable. I didn't stop to consider how my actions affected my mum or others. It was about me. I felt like a caged lion. Everything around me seemed oppressive.

> In righteousness you shall be established; you shall be far from oppression, for you shall not fear; and from terror, for it shall not come near you. (Isaiah 54:14)

If there is a spirit assigned to different nations, "How you are fallen from heaven, o Lucifer, son of the morning! How you are cut down to the ground, you who weakened the nations!" (Isaiah 14:12). The one who ruled England did not favor me.

I returned home, having missed my sister's Christine's wedding by about ten days. She got married to that lovely boy, Mick, we all adored. How could she or anyone imagine that just a month before the wedding, a terrible tragedy in our family would take place. Nevertheless, they went ahead with their plans. After all, it would never be the right time, not after this. I was thankful I did not have to be there. God had spared me from being there when the news of Jimmy came to my sisters, my brother, and—most of all—my mum. Later, I learned that our doctor was called and asked to come to our house to be there when my mother came home and heard the tragic news. The doctor was ready to administer the right sedatives. She passed out.

Once more in London, I went back to my last employer, who gave me a job willingly. I was back in the hustle and bustle of London living, working, going dancing with the girls, and meeting new boys. I wasn't too interested, but what else was there? I don't remember if I thought of Jesus very often. I mean, He was always there for me, and I went back to church, but I wasn't talking to Him much.

> Call upon Me, and I will answer you, and show you great and mighty things, which you do not know. (Jeremiah 33:3)

But I didn't think that He would leave me. I never knew His Word or His promises because I had never laid hands on a Bible. Was it possible to know Him if I didn't know what He said? Later, I learned that Jesus is known as the Word.

> In the beginning was the Word, the Word was with God, the Word was God. (John 1:1)

But I didn't have the Word. Did that mean I didn't have Jesus?

> I have declared the former thing from the beginning;
> They went forth from My mouth…(Isaiah 48:3)

But I had never read His Word, so how could I hear Him? I didn't hear from Terry often, but when I did, it was well worth the wait. His letters always made me realize how much I missed him and wanted to be with him. Time went on, and I found myself longing to go. Nothing interested me. I was still searching for an identity.

4

Chapter

CONFUSION

TERRY WROTE TO me and asked if I would meet him in Canada, as it wasn't possible for me to get into the States. He was going to take a motorcycle trip with his brother—they planned to travel to the west coast of Canada—and he wondered if I would like to go along. I didn't hesitate for a moment; the answer was yes! But how was I to get away? I didn't want to hurt the person that I was dating. Was there another way?

Jesus, could You please help me? I prayed. *Do You have any hope or a future for me?*

> For I know the thoughts that I think toward you, says
> the Lord, thoughts of peace and not of evil, to give you
> a future and a hope. (Jeremiah 29:11)

I told my boyfriend that I was leaving. He thought that I would return, but in June 1975, I left my home for good—or so it seemed at the time. I would return eventually but never to live there permanently again. My mother used to say that London was not good for me. It was true. In London, I always felt as if there was a ceiling just above my head that I couldn't break through. The one time I'd gone to America with Terry, however, I had a strong sense of being *home*.

Now the Lord is Spirit and where the Spirit of the Lord
is there is freedom. (2 Corinthians 3:17)

Before I left London, I had to make some arrangements. I needed
to establish a base in Canada. My sister, Barbara, had a friend who lived
in Canada. She'd come to stay at our house once. She and her husband
later emigrated from Scotland to Saint Catherine's, which was not
far from Toronto. Maybe she would allow me to stay. My sister kindly
contacted her, and she was willing to let me stay. So there I was, living
in Saint Catherine's, waiting for Terry and his brother. They eventually
came, and we traveled to the western part of Canada.

I am very sure there was something I needed to tell my Scottish
friends before I left, but I didn't know what that was.

For the next two or three years, Terry and I had an on-and-off
relationship due to my rebellion and his stubbornness.

For rebellion is as the sin of witchcraft, and stubbornness
is as iniquity and idolatry. (1 Samuel 15.23)

When it was time for Terry to get back to work, our relationship
suffered a huge strain because I couldn't get into America legally. I went
home numerous times. I managed to get a fiancée visa, which afforded
us a few months to decide whether to get married. In my heart, I didn't
like the idea of the government telling me when to get married. I felt
that Terry would think I married him just to get into America, and that
was never the case. So I decided to try something else.

While staying with my Scottish friends, they often drove across the
Niagara Falls border on Sundays to buy alcohol in America. The bars
in Canada were closed, and it was a very normal occurrence for those
who wanted to drink on a Sunday to cross over the border into America.
I was considering coming into America illegally. What was I thinking,
or was I thinking at all? I wonder what Jesus would have said.

"If you love Me, keep My commandments… (John 14:15)

I thought I did love Jesus. But I didn't know anything about His commandments. So for now I will do things *my way*. One Sunday evening, with Terry on his motorcycle and I in my friend's car, we drove into America.

At the border, the border patrol asked where we were going, and he asked Jim about their citizenship in Canada. Then he pointed at me and said, "What about you?"

Margaret answered, "She's visiting us."

Was this really me? This wasn't how I was taught to do things. I was not only breaking the law of the land, but I was also breaking God's law.

> Let every soul be subject to the governing authorities. For there is no authority except from God, and the authorities that exist are appointed by God. Therefore whoever resists the authority resists the ordinance of God, and those who resist will bring judgement on themselves. (Romans 13:1–2)

I had brought judgment on myself. I had become a criminal. I was someone who had committed a crime and deserved to pay the penalty.

> Enter by the narrow gate; for wide is the gate and broad is the way that leads to destruction, and there are many who go in by it. (Matthew 7:13)

As I look back on that time in my life, I now can see that I was headed on the broad road that leads to destruction. I had never heard of the narrow way because I always did life *my way*.

I didn't hear from Jesus and didn't know what He thought about this. It had been at least twenty years since He was in my bedroom, when it seemed as though I knew Him. But I didn't hear from Him when all of those loved ones died. Why did He let them die? Was there something that I needed to know? If so, what was it?

> Behold, the Lord's Hand is not shortened, that it cannot save; Nor His ear heavy, that it cannot hear. But your iniquities have separated you from your God; and your sins have hidden His face from you, so that He will not hear. (Isaiah 59:1–2)

I was now with Terry in America. And I was always looking over my shoulder.

> For there is nothing covered, that shall not be revealed; nor hidden, that shall not be known. (Luke 12:2)

We traveled across the country and would stop in places where Terry knew he could find work as a union member. By 1976 he was working in Long Island for the local newspaper, and I worked for a wonderful Irish American family—a doctor, his wife, and their eleven children. I cleaned their fifteen-room Dutch colonial house, which sat in a lovely part of Long Island. I found a church and would often go and talk to Jesus. I always talked to Him, but He never seemed to answer me.

> If anyone does not abide in Me, he is cast out as a branch and is withered … (John 15:6)

I just couldn't settle. I knew that I wasn't living the right way, but who was? I wasn't the only sinner in the world. Still, this heaviness would not leave me.

> Why are you cast down, O my soul? And why are you disquieted within me? (Psalm 42:5)

I decided to make an appointment to talk with the priest. This was all I knew to do. I supposed a priest was the closest I could get to God.

> For there is one God and one mediator between God
> and men, the Man Christ Jesus … (1 Timothy 2:5)

The priest was kind but gave no advice. How could he advise me when I didn't know what was wrong? I knew that I was not living morally the way I should. My small apartment was really just a guise to make everything look decent. But I was a liar, a hypocrite, because in reality, I was living with Terry. We both seemed happy, but I couldn't justify my lifestyle. I was in the country illegally and had too much rebellion in me to be content.

One day after a big argument, Terry and I parted ways. I took a Greyhound bus to Albuquerque, where I knew I could get work. I didn't talk to Terry for months, not until Christmas 1977, when I called him. I supposed Christmas was a time when you wanted to be with someone you cared for. He had been living in Texas, working for a newspaper. He had many drinking partners at his work and seemed to like the lifestyle. When we talked on the phone, he asked me to come for a visit. I was happy to be on the go again.

So just before Christmas, we met at a Greyhound bus station, where Terry always seemed to be picking me up. It was good to see him, and it seemed that I fit right into his life in Houston, like hand in glove. I began living the Houston lifestyle, which entailed work and going out with friends, drinking and dancing, and looking for an identity.

> But take heed to yourselves, lest your hearts be weighed
> down with carousing, drunkenness, and cares of this
> life, and the day come upon you unexpectantly. (Luke
> 21:34)

Terry and I were back together, and I thought maybe this could work out after all. Terry gave up smoking cigarettes but not pot. Why did I go back to Terry? Proverbs 1:7 says, "The fear of the Lord is the beginning of knowledge, but fools despise wisdom and instruction." I was not ready to listen to any instruction. I would do things my way. I knew that Terry had a few insecurities, as I did. I used to think that he was so different from my dad. He was less boisterous, but was he really so different from my dad? Did I go back to Terry because I was trying to find and fix my dad? This familiar circumstance, even though it wasn't good for me, felt safe. It was all I knew. But it was not who I was called to be.

> Fear not, for I am with you; Be not dismayed, for I am your God. I will strengthen you, yes, I will help you, I will uphold you with My righteous right hand. (Isaiah 41:10)

From a very young age, I had watched my dad, whom I loved, get drunk and be so much less than what he was created to be. Was I becoming like my mother? I heard that her hair went white overnight—my dad had done something to cause that. Was I headed on that same path? Was I going to wash my hands (like Pilate) of the whole situation? These were questions that I did not broach at the time. I didn't want to look at them. I just wanted to enjoy being young and living life as carefree as possible. I closed my eyes.

> I will bring the blind by a way they did not know; I will lead them in paths they have not known. I will make darkness light before them, and crooked paths straight. These things I will do for them, and not forsake them. (Isaiah 42:16)

I just wanted to be happy. But how could I be? I was living a lie. It was late November 1978 when Terry said to me, out of the blue, "Let's get married!"

I answered, "Okay." Why no struggle? I don't know. It just seemed like the right time. However, thoughts of my brother Jimmy always haunted me. What was the use of marriage? What if I married Terry, and we decided it was the wrong thing to do? I'd always thought of marriage as the end of a person's life, as if living stopped then, and everything became mundane and boring. But somehow, I brushed those thoughts out of my mind and mustered the courage to walk through life without running away.

The next day, we went to the courthouse during my lunch hour (Terry worked nights), wearing jeans and T-shirts. It was Monday, November 22 1978. We were ushered in to the justice of the peace, who asked if we wanted a long or short ceremony. We replied in unison, "Short!" He then said, "I pronounce you man and wife." We both responded by getting up and bumping into one another. I went back to work. I didn't mention anything to anyone and just carried on as usual. So we were married, and I was still the same person. Nothing drastic happened—yet.

Terry was still at the newspaper, and I worked at an employment agency. Yes, I was back in the employment business. I worked for a woman who owned two agencies in the Houston area. The building where I worked housed a few other small businesses. One happened to be a small talent agency. One afternoon, a young talent scout named Steve came to tell me that he was looking for a few people to man booths at a weekend spiritual festival in Houston, and he needed a person for the astrology booth.

"Do you know anything about astrology?" he asked.

"Yes, of course I do." I was happy to oblige, and of course, the one hundred dollars a day made it more agreeable.

> And take heed, lest you lift your eyes to heaven, and
> when you see the sun, the moon and the stars, all the
> host of heaven, you feel driven to worship them and
> serve them … (Deuteronomy 4:19)

When I arrived at the festival, I learned that someone already had been assigned the astrology booth, so Steve said to me, "I really need your help. Will you man the palm reading booth?"

As it happened, I had read enough about palm reading to be able to get by, so I said yes. One of the first ladies I saw at the booth had been through a very serious heart operation—I saw it. I wondered if she had told other people what I had said because that evening, when it was time to leave, I couldn't get away because of the number of people lined up, waiting for me to read their palms. I seemed to know about them as I touched their hands. Was this a gift that God had given me? Was I using this gift in the wrong way?

At the end of the night, a lady spoke to all the participants and said that she had sensed a strong presence there. She wanted all of us to attend a meeting the following week. What was that presence she sensed? What would the meeting be about?

> For though we walk in the flesh, we do not walk
> according to the flesh, for the weapons of our warfare
> are not carnal but mighty in God for the pulling down
> of strongholds. (2 Corinthians 10:3-4)

I thought I had something to tell this lady. *When I know what it is,* I thought, *I should tell her. Something about strongholds.* Was I opening up myself to strongholds?

At work the following week, I talked about the weekend to my boss, who happened to be a Christian. She was adamant that I should not go to that meeting, saying that all of this was the devil's work. I wasn't sure that I agreed with that. Surely this was just harmless fun.

I thought back to my days in Torquay, England, and I remembered how Cosy (another Christian) had become very upset over these things. Why was she so upset?

I appreciated my boss's concern; I hadn't planned to go to that meeting anyway. We never discussed it again.

5

Chapter

CHANGES

L IFE IN HOUSTON continued, and on most Saturdays, Terry
worked, and I would go to the gym with my friend. One Saturday
afternoon at the gym, I began to get terrible pains in my stomach. I
passed something, and immediately the pain subsided. Eventually, I
saw a doctor, and the consensus was that I'd had a miscarriage. I didn't
take this too seriously, as the thought of having children hadn't entered
my mind. In the ensuing days, I began to crave my mum's stew, yet I
felt sort of sick. Again, I saw a doctor. He told me I was pregnant. Terry
and I were going to be parents. The thought was extremely sobering
to me. I was about to get very serious. I wanted my child to be brought
up properly. I didn't want a life of drinking and partying. This child
deserved a decent moral upbringing. But that was easier said than done.
Terry and I were not the picture-perfect role models.

Terry's mother was not happy that I was pregnant. My mother
commented that I might have been having twins if indeed that was a
miscarriage previously—another sobering thought. My due date was
March 31, 1980. We were always very active, and in November 1979,
around Thanksgiving, Terry and I took a thirteen-mile hike in Big Bend
National Park, the only place in Texas where there are real mountains.
I did really well, but upon finishing the hike, I began to get pains, as if

the baby was going to come. To be on the safe side, I saw the doctor the following week. He said he thought that my due date was wrong because the baby seemed bigger than usual. They did an ultrasound.

I joked, "Don't tell me I'm having twins."

The nurse replied, "I'm not supposed to tell you, but the doctor will come in and see you in a moment."

He came in, looked at the ultrasound, and said, "Well, Mrs. Phillips, you have two babies in there."

Two? Two babies at once? Deep in my soul, I knew this was orchestrated by the hand of Jesus.

> Before I formed you in the womb I knew you; before you
> were born I sanctified you ... (Jeremiah 1:5)

When I finally saw Terry, he noticed the expression on my face and said, "What is wrong?"

"Oh, nothing. There are two babies in here."

Terry responded, "Neat!"

Funny, but the parking lot seemed to have grown, and it took a long time to find our car. We were quiet. This was no longer just about us. In those days, doctors recommended that women who were having multiple births should take off from work six weeks prior to the due date. I was reluctant to leave my job and the wonderful people with whom I worked. But I was getting bigger, and it was becoming physically uncomfortable. I would have to let go of other things too.

Life had been about me and what I wanted to do. In my spare time, I loved my tap and jazz dance classes and my acting lessons. I studied acting under Chris, a woman who was well known in Houston. She told me that she had scheduled me for a part in a play at a dinner theater in downtown Houston. Rehearsals were to start in April. The play would star Mel Ferrer, and I would play the English maid. I couldn't have been more elated. I had never gotten so close to something that I wanted. Was this the identity that I was looking for? Maybe I could lose myself in each different character I played.

But when Chris learned that I was pregnant—and with twins—she felt it would be impossible for me to play the part. She would find someone else. I begged her to allow me to have my babies and still play the part, but she would not relent. She was much wiser than I, but I was devastated. The direction of my life was now being altered, and there was nothing I could do. Maybe my life was not to be about me and my exploits. I wondered how much of my life I would have to give up.

> Yes, and if I am being poured out as a drink offering ...
> (Philippians 2:17)

My mum said she would come to be with us while I gave birth to her grandsons—I knew the babies were boys. There was no doubt; I knew them. Terry's mum would later join us.

Around one in the morning on Sunday, March 16, I started feeling cramps. Terry wasn't home yet. He worked nights and typically went out with his coworkers for a drink after work. I was angry, disliking his lifestyle, and that anger only made the cramps come on faster. This time I couldn't run. This time I had others to consider. It was no longer just about me. I had to dig deeper inside myself to find the strength.

By eight in the morning, I was ready to go to the hospital with Terry—with our mums in tow. The rain was very heavy that day. The fish must have been biting because from a very young age, these young men would love to fish.

> Then He said to them, "Follow Me, and I will make you
> fishers of men." (Matthew 4:19)

I find it interesting that in Matthew 4:18, Jesus is walking by the Sea of Galilee, and He sees two brothers—Peter and Andrew—casting their net into the sea. When Jesus spoke to them (the words of Matthew 4:19), they dropped their nets and followed Him. And going on from there, He saw two other brothers, James and John. Two sets of brothers in just four verses. I think the Lord orchestrated this scripture to be spoken over our boys. Deep in my soul, I knew that they were called to be disciples of Jesus, fishers of men (humankind).

A long day ensued with much pain.

> And to the woman He said: "I will greatly multiply your sorrow and your conception; In pain you shall bring forth children; your desire shall be for your husband, And he shall rule over you." (Genesis 3:16)

During labor I thought, *Millions of women have done this over the years. I'm sure I can too.* The nurses put a monitor inside me to check the babies' heartbeats, and then a nurse said, "Oh, you have a boy and a girl—one heartbeat is faster than the other."

Immediately I turned to Terry and said, "Not true; they are both boys." I knew them!

Everything seemed to be going well, but the hospital staff didn't agree, and without asking me, they brought in an anesthesiologist and stuck a needle in my lower back. From the waist down, I went completely numb. It was called a saddle-block. The nurses said it wasn't every day that a woman gave birth to twins. The doctor proceeded to pull out my babies. The first one who came into the world would be called James, after my dad and my brother. His middle name would be Lee, after Terry's dad. The second baby was actually tap dancing on my right side; he was trapped and couldn't get into position, as James was already there. His name would be Daniel (my favorite name); his middle name would be Carl (Terry's favorite uncle—and almost my name). I suppose the epidural took away any pain that I would have felt from having babies the natural way, on my own. The doctor began to pull our first baby out of my womb, and my body raised off the bed. I couldn't feel a thing. At 5:30 p.m. on Sunday, March 16, James entered this world very bruised. Daniel, looking much less bruised, was on James's heels, arriving six minutes later. James weighed five pounds, five ounces; and Daniel weighed five pounds—two beautiful baby boys. The nurses laid them both on my chest, and it was like I had always known them, and my job was to tell them what I needed to tell them—when I knew what that was.

Terry still worked for the newspaper, but just after James and Daniel were born, my ex-boss, having connections in the local area, got him an interview at the post office. He took the test and passed with flying colors. He is naturally clever. So he began his new career, working for the United States Post Office. Looking back, it is not hard to see that the hand of God was in that move. Working at the post office wasn't Terry's dream job, but he was being moved away from the newspaper and all his drinking buddies. We lived just outside of Houston, where we rented a three-bedroom house. There we were—Terry, James, Daniel, Nellie my cockatiel, my rabbit, and I. Both our mothers stayed to help with the babies. They got along very well with each other and were a great help to me. Before my mother left to go home, she asked if Terry and I would consider getting married in the church under the hand of God. No one else, just us. We said okay.

On that morning, Terry and I stood in front of the priest, each of us holding one of the boys, while my mum enthusiastically handed the priest twenty dollars to perform the wedding ceremony. He had us repeat the marriage vows after him. This was serious. Could we fulfill this commitment? Time would tell.

Terry now was working full time at the post office but began to work a part-time job, just to make ends meet. I knew deep down that soon I would have to contribute. I had always worked, and I didn't think it was possible for me to be a stay-at-home mum. One afternoon, Terry came home from work and found me sitting in between my mum and his. The babies were being taken care of. He made it clear that we could not manage if I didn't work. This became a heated topic between us. Although my heart was extremely heavy when I thought of leaving my babies, I began to look for work—on the condition that I would work only part-time while the boys were so young.

My first interview was with a family-owned publishers' representative's company in Houston, headquartered in northern California. The job title was part-time marketing director, and the job description asked for someone who could make "cold calls on phone with the aim of selling prospective advertisers to buy advertising space in several industrial magazines." These magazines covered a wide array of industries, such as welding, engineering, mining, and the like. This satellite office was managed by a very kind, seemingly religious elderly gentleman. I got the job. He made one request—that I use both my first and middle names (after all, I was in Texas), so I was known as Carole Ann.

I was suddenly in the world of print advertising sales and the good-ole-boy network of Texas. I found a good babysitter who looked after my boys from 7:30 a.m. until noon, five days a week. This was extremely hard for me. Although I liked working, my heart was always very heavy when I dropped off my babies and ran off to work. I would think, *Why do people like me bring babies into this world and then have someone else take care of them?* I had a longing in my heart for more time with my children; it was a heavy yoke for me. It was a feeling in my heart that never left me.

> And everyone who has left houses or brothers or sisters or father or mother or wife or children or lands, for My names sake, shall receive a hundredfold, and inherit eternal life. (Matthew 19:29)

My job went very well, and I had a few write-ups in publishers' newsletters. I was given a company car. Then one day, I was told that the company really needed help in Glendale, California. Although I flippantly said I should move to California to help boost the Glendale office, the owners responded to that notion with a resounding yes! They made it clear that they would pay for the entire move for me and my family. Terry said he would try to get a transfer. I felt that if this was meant to be, Terry would get a transfer, and we would go.

The people that we knew in Texas, however, thought we were crazy. They collectively said, "Don't go to California. It's full of cults, and you guys have your children to think of." Little did they know that the omnipresent Lord Jesus the Christ is in Southern California as well as Texas and beyond.

Terry got a transfer to a post office thirty miles from where I would be working. So then we had to find a place to live. In February 1983, Terry and I flew to Los Angeles. We stayed with friends of Terry's parents in Costa Mesa—John, an army chaplain, and Mae, his wife. They were a beautiful Christian family who began to pray for us. Terry's parents came to stay with the boys while we were gone. That was the first time I had ever left my babies; they were almost three years old.

I hoped our lifestyle would change for the better, but there were still the occasional drunken parties, and Terry was still smoking pot as he pleased (though not around the children). At this point, I was not close to Terry. We seemed to be on different roads in life. I didn't respect him, and I'm sure he felt the same way about me, but he never said much—ever. We drove up from Costa Mesa to San Dimas each morning, both awestruck by the beauty of the white mountain peaks (in those days, winter would bring snow to Southern California). Within the week, we found a house to rent in a very nice part of the city. We secured a preschool for boys that had a swimming pool. They were my water babies—they loved the water. Our job was done, and we flew back to Houston.

On March 4, 1983, our little family "marched forth" to our new life in California.

6

Chapter

DISTRACTIONS

B OTH TERRY AND I were earning a good wage, so we began to look for a house to buy in the local area. My job was going very well. I had secured a major account for one of the more popular magazines. I was also doing very well on the other magazines that I represented. L.A. was more visible than Texas, so our office received a lot of visits from our publishers. My job became very demanding. The better I did, the better I had to do. I didn't need a manager; I put enough pressure on myself. My prideful ego had to win. This market was big, and there was a lot of business to be had, and I was the ideal person to go get it. I was striving to be the best that I could be. I was torn between the pursuit of winning and just being. Could I just be? Could I just be still? Psalm 46:10 says, "Be still and know that I Am God," but I wasn't sure that I could. In my heart, I yearned to be home when my children got home from school—to have the time to bake cookies, to be more involved, to leisurely read stories to them. That time never came. I was already mired in my work life.

Life was extremely demanding. I thought I was strong and capable and could do it all, but could I?

> For what has man for all his labor, and for the striving of
> his heart with which he has toiled under the sun? For all
> his days are sorrowful, and his work burdensome; even
> in the night his heart takes no rest. This also is vanity.
> (Ecclesiastes 2:22–23)

My ego strove to win. By July 1983, I began to feel different in my body. Over the weeks I'd noticed a change in my weight; my tummy seemed bigger. *Surely I can't be pregnant!* I thought. After a thorough checkup, I was told that I *was* pregnant and two to three months along. I hate to write this now, but at the time, I was not happy at this news. Little did I know that this little baby that Jesus began to knit in my womb (along with James and Daniel) would bring an abundant life to me. And as my children grew, there was something that I knew I must teach them; it was of the utmost importance.

> Train up a child in the way he should go, and when he
> is old he will not depart from it. (Proverbs 22:6)

Upon hearing the news, I contacted my superiors and explained what was happening. They were absolutely wonderful and told me that I was to go and come as I needed, and that if I needed to work from home when the baby arrived, that would be fine. I continued working—hard. The baby was due in February 1984. We never thought, when we were looking for a house the previous February, that in exactly a year we would have another addition to our family. Days were long. On two occasions while pregnant, I nearly passed out, particularly when I was around a lot of people. This seemed strange, as I normally thrived around a lot of people. When I was pregnant, though, I felt overwhelmed and faint. The doctor said that the baby was probably lying on a nerve.

In those days, the doctor couldn't tell us the sex of the baby, but I thought we probably had another boy. My doctor had no firm due date for me. He said, "If the baby isn't here by January 29, then I want you in here early on Thursday morning, February 2." (Later, I heard that the doctor had a golf tournament that weekend. Couldn't miss that to deliver my baby.) My mother-in-law said that she had never seen a woman go to the hospital with no sign of labor. She was right, but I was trusting in the doctor, and I didn't question anything—neither did Terry. They began to induce me at 6:30 a.m. on February 2. I struggled with the idea that the baby was being disrupted, seemingly early.

Terry spoke to the nurses and said that we wanted to see the doctor. They said, "No, the doctor wants you in here today."

Throughout the day, the pains became heavier and heavier. Labor had begun, and eventually I was wheeled into the delivery room.

> A woman, when she is in labor, has sorrow because her hour has come; but as soon as she has given birth to the child, she no longer remembers the anguish, for the joy that a human being has been born into the world. (John 16:21)

The doctor began to deliver our baby. No sooner had the baby been taken out of my womb than I heard, "Congratulations. You have a baby girl." They showed her to us, very briefly, and then snatched her away. Something wasn't right. I only glanced at a little baby with a mop of black hair. *What's happening?* I wondered. I was due to have my tubes tied as soon as she was delivered. Maybe I would decide not get my tubes tied if something was wrong with our baby. We were then told that our baby was having a hard time breathing. She had to be put in an incubator. She was also jaundiced. The battle had begun.

> For You formed my inward parts, You covered me in my mother's womb, I will praise You, for I am fearfully and wonderfully made; marvelous are Your works, and that my soul knows very well. My frame was not hidden from You, when I was made in secret … (Psalm 139:13, 15)

I remembered that about a month or so earlier, my mother-in-law had asked if I would go with her to a charismatic meeting at the local Catholic church. I was surprised, as she was a born-again Christian, not Catholic. She had read in the local newspaper that a charismatic, spirit-filled priest would be there. He was renowned for his healing hands. Many who were touched by him had been healed of cancer and other illnesses. I said I would go.

While there, I began to weep profusely. I always wept at church, but not like this. It was hard to control myself. A woman took one of my hands, and my mother-in-law took my other. They walked me up to the altar. I didn't look up; I just bowed my head and wept. I felt someone put an arm at my back, as to keep me from falling. It was the priest. He touched my stomach, where Angela (named for my mother) was growing in my womb. Suddenly, I felt a powerful surge of heat travel to my stomach—something I had never felt before and have never felt since. I don't know what was prayed over Angela and me. I was sobbing profusely. There was an obvious, beautiful warmth and the sense of humility. Jesus was with us, and He was at work. Was the Holy Spirit sealing Angela? Later, I would learn that the Holy Spirit was given to believers as a guarantee—down payment—to assure us that our full inheritance as children of God will be delivered.

The Holy Spirit confirms that we belong to God, as 2 Corinthians 5:5 tells us, "Now He who has prepared us for this very thing is God, who also has given us the Spirit as a guarantee." I went to see Angela in her incubator, but I wasn't allowed to hold her. How could she get better without the touch of her mother? I overheard a conversation outside of my hospital room. The pediatrician asked the gynecologist, "What is wrong with the Phillips baby, just immature?" The reply was, "Yes, she was delivered too early. Her lungs were not fully developed."

In the incubator she wore a white cap (which I have kept to this day) and a pair of sunglasses—that's all. We jokingly called her our Hollywood star. She was not happy; she cried a lot, and I was dying inside. I remembered that warmth I'd felt when the Holy Spirit touched

Angela in my womb. *We will win this battle,* I thought. I didn't call any of my family in London. I wasn't giving in because I knew without a shadow of a doubt that Jesus would heal her.

At this time the couple that we stayed with in Costa Mesa came to see us. Chaplain John and Mae prayed over Angela. I was very vocal in saying that I knew that Jesus would heal her. I had *no* doubt.

Mae said, "With the faith of her mother, this baby will thrive."

> But without faith it is impossible to please Him, for he who comes to God must believe that He is, and that He is a rewarder of those who diligently seek Him. (Hebrews 11:6)

Within days, I was standing at the incubator, talking to Angela, when my pediatrician came in and almost commanded the nurse, "Take that baby out of the incubator and give her to her mother." I finally held Angela and breastfed her. She was content and began to grow strong. I was thankful for my pediatrician. It seemed that he had heard from the Lord. I later learned that he became an Episcopalian priest. I believe that the Lord had spoken to him. Jesus knew Angela.

> Before I formed you in the womb I knew you; Before you were born, I sanctified you … —Jeremiah 1:5

7
Chapter

STRIVING

W E FOUND A house but not in the immediate area. We were advised that it was more affordable to buy in an area fifteen miles away in a community that was estimated to grow within the next ten to fifteen years. So we did. Angela was almost four months old when we moved. The boys had just turned four years. I still worked from home so I could be with Angela and be there for the boys when they came home from preschool. On the occasions when I needed to meet a customer face-to-face, I secured a babysitter for just a few hours. James and Daniel went to a Christian preschool until they were old enough to start public school. Angela followed suit.

Terry had the children involved in sports. Each of them had their special sport and special interests. James and Daniel played baseball; Angela, soccer. Yes, Jesus had healed Angela's lungs before she left the hospital. Terry was an excellent coach and dad. He was very tough on the boys, but they were hard to handle at times. They had a lot of energy and didn't listen, except to each other, and that is still true to this day. I didn't help matters, as I didn't want to listen. The boys were about four when they said they wanted to fish, and they loved it. Even older men would ask them what bait they were using. I knew that Jesus knew!

When they got older, they began to teach themselves to surf, and to this day, they surf, fish, and play softball on a team.

Angela was a snow-boarder and an excellent soccer player—so much so that it gave me a love for the game. She earned a college scholarship but declined it. As a wife and mother, she sometimes still plays soccer.

My job soon came to an end, as I left for a very challenging position. The man I worked with had mentioned my name at an advertising representatives meeting. He told the recruiter that I was "effective." I pondered on that word and tried to see myself as effective. Was I effective at making the company money? Probably. Effective at building good, strong, long-lasting business relationships? Probably. Effective at having integrity and building trust? Probably. But how effective was I at home? Was I an effective mother and wife? How effective was I when things didn't work out quite as I had hoped?

This is something for everyone to ask themselves. How effective are we when we would prefer to be doing something else? At the time, it seemed that life would have been much easier for the whole family if I had not been recruited by a high-powered company. It was January 1986. Angela about to be two years old; the boys would soon be six. I was selling advertising space into four of the major weekly news magazines, among other upscale, yuppie-type magazines. My office was in Orange County. In the mornings, it took over an hour to get there, and normally, it took up to two hours to get home. I was hired into a senior sales position. It was continually intimated to me that I was now in the "major leagues." The company was a Fortune 500 company, and the benefit package was very good. I had a brand-new company car every two years, all expenses paid. It may sound good, but this took a big toll on me and our family. I was gone for a long period during the day. The job took a 150 percent commitment. I had to secure a full-time babysitter for Angela, which was extremely difficult and agonizing. The one I found, from my church, ended up fracturing Angela's ankle, and she had to have a cast. The whole ordeal was too much for me to bear. I couldn't do it. I called my poor mother, now seventy-three years old, and begged her to come and help me with Angela. She obliged.

I told Terry that if he wanted me to do this job, he would have to change his work schedule and be home by the time the boys came home from school. That meant that his day started at four in the morning, sometimes earlier. But he was okay with it. He wanted me to do this. Financially, it was good. Terry invested wisely, and I thank him for it today.

We began to juggle our young family. Terry worked awkward hours, and I tried to make it all work properly, tried to make everyone happy as much as possible. This company invested a lot in their sales people. I had to travel to other states and go through very expensive training with my peers. I felt different from my peers. I was spontaneous and genuine, but this was not what management wanted. They had a proven technique that worked, and I was not following suit very well. On training days, we trainees were videotaped performing mock presentations. They wanted us to present the product the way they wanted us to. To me, it was canned, and I just could not do it. Management was phony; I was real. I wondered if I was upsetting their apple cart. I began to falter. I was so intimidated, so frightened of failing. I had built a brick wall around me so high that I didn't know who I was anymore. It's true that I had my health and healthy children; I had a good job. Maybe this was the straw that broke the camel's back. To my soul, it felt like a fiery furnace because I was being stripped of my mask—the hypocrisy that I had hidden behind. This mask had protected me, or so I thought. But now each layer was slowly but surely being peeled away.

> Therefore, laying aside all malice, all deceit, hypocrisy,
> envy, and evil speaking as newborn babes, desire the
> pure milk of the word, that you may grow thereby ...
> (1 Peter 2:1-2)

Soon the world would see me for what I truly was—a pretender. I wasn't the confident person I portrayed myself to be. This job needed individuals who were comfortable stepping over others to get what they wanted. I, on the other hand, felt ill-equipped to do the job. I felt so vulnerable, and I didn't like that feeling. I thought, *How can I live if others watch me fail?* I thought back to my brother Jimmy. Was this how he felt? Like a failure? I wanted to run. It would have made everything so much easier. But I didn't want to let my husband down. Also, I couldn't admit to myself that I could not do this. I felt trapped. I hated being so unhappy. I yearned to be joyful and happy, but it seemed there was a dark cloud hanging over me. Even when I came home to my family, I brought the ugliness of the job with me. Life was overwhelming, and I was losing grip of my false image, grip of my false bravado, grip of the rope that I was holding, grip of myself. I was at a pivotal point in my life—a crossroads. Should I take the narrow road or the broad road?

Where was Jesus in all of this? Had I strayed so far from Him? Had I run from Jesus? Up until now, I had run away from anything I didn't like or didn't want to face. If I didn't like a job, I would leave it. If I wasn't happy at home in London, I would go. If I wasn't fully ready to make a commitment to marriage, I would run. But this time, something was telling me to stay and face it.

> I will give you a new heart and put a new spirit within you; I will take the heart of stone out of your flesh and give you a heart of flesh. I will put My Spirit within you and cause you to walk in My statutes and you will keep My judgements and do them. (Ezekiel 36:26–27)

Oh, how I wanted to run, but I couldn't. Instead, I was being moved to stay and keep walking through the dark tunnel.

> Your ears shall hear a word behind you, saying, "This is the way, walk in it." (Isaiah 30:21)

It reminded me of being a small child and longing to go with Jesus. Yet even then, I knew that I had to walk this journey. Now, it seemed that my natural eyes were blind. I could not see, but I knew that must keep walking.

> I will bring the blind by a way they did not know, I will lead them in paths they have not known. I will make darkness light before them and make crooked paths straight. These things I will do for them, and not forsake them. (Isaiah 42:16)

Driving to work in the mornings, I would feel drowsy, like I wanted to sleep. It probably was depression setting in. I was searching for the proverbial light at the end of a dark tunnel. But who or what was that light?

> Then Jesus spoke to them again, saying, "I am the light of the world. He who follows Me shall not walk in darkness, but have the light of life" (John 8:12)

I thought back to the wooden picture that sat on the mantel in my bedroom, the one with the closed door; the one with Jesus knocking on the door with no handle. Would Jesus open that door and let me run through it?

> I am the door, if anyone enters by Me, he will be saved …
> —John 10:9

8

Chapter

AWAKENING

THE MORNING WAS just like any other morning. I was driving to
work when I came across a radio program that featured a preacher
speaking. He had a silly sense of humor, which made me laugh. I
continued to listen. A day or two later, as I listened to his program again,
this preacher said something that made me think. It was as if he were
sitting in my car. He asked, "Do you know Jesus?"

I answered—with an attitude, "Of course I know Jesus. I am [my
religion]." All through that day, though, I felt as if I was being asked a
question, but I couldn't answer in the affirmative. The question was,
"Do you know what Jesus said?" My mind clung to that question. I did
not know what Jesus said. Then how could I know Him? But surely, I
knew Him. What about all the times in my life that I asked Him for
help, and He usually answered? Well, maybe not always. Maybe He
didn't answer when all those people I loved died, but I still thought I
knew Him. Or did I just know of Him? I continued to limp and stagger
through this dark tunnel, but within a week or so, I came to the end of
it—the end of the tunnel, the end of my rope, and the end of myself. I
screamed out to God—the God I thought I knew as a child; Jesus, who
died on the cross. Sobbing, I screamed out to Him, "I cannot do this
anymore!" I was broken. I let go of the rope. I surrendered. I gave up

doing it my way. Surrender felt as though I was hanging off of a cliff with no other recourse but to trust in Jesus to catch me – He did!

> Behold, I will do a new thing, now it shall spring forth;
> Shall you not know it? I will even make a road in the
> wilderness and rivers in the desert. (Isaiah 43:19)

I suddenly realized what I had done; it was as if everything I had done panned before my eyes.

> And if they are bound in fetters, held in the cords of
> affliction, then He tells them their work and their
> transgressions - that they have acted defiantly. He also
> opens their ears to instruction, and commands that they
> turn from iniquity. (Job 36:8-10)

Later, I learned that the Bible speaks about books that have recorded everything a person has done in his or her lifetime—all that each of us thought or did.

> And I saw the dead, small and great, standing before
> God, and books were opened, and another book was
> opened, which is the Book of Life, And the dead were
> judged according to their works, by the things which
> were written in the books. (Revelation 20:12)

So this book contains each person's every thought, every word, and every deed. We each have our own book at the throne of God, awaiting judgment day.

> A fiery stream issued and came forth from Him. A
> thousand thousands ministered to Him; Ten thousand
> times ten thousand stood before Him. The court was
> seated, and the books were opened. (Daniel 7:10)

I realized how sinful I was. My book was filled with sin. I saw my rebellion. I saw the pride. I saw the fornication. I saw that I had gone against God in every way possible. The arrogant recklessness of one who would illegally cross the American border. The spiritual prostitution of idolatry, astrology, palm reading, and mediums is witchcraft. Leviticus 19:31 tells us, "Give no regard to mediums and familiar spirits, do not seek after them, to be defiled by them: I am the LORD your God." I had done things my way. My sin had separated me from a holy God. I was extremely sorry and begged Jesus to forgive me.

> The Lord is not slack concerning His promise, as some count slackness, but is longsuffering towards us, not willing that any should perish but that all should come to repentance. (2 Peter 3:9)

I repented of all of my sin. Later, I learned that to *repent* means to turn from sin and walk away from it, to want to change. Repenting isn't just being sorry for getting caught but truly being sorry, to the point of changing your mind and turning from sin. I suddenly had a clear understanding that I would be in heaven with Jesus one day. I was certain of that, not because of anything I had done but because of what Jesus had done on the cross at Calvary more than two thousand years ago.

> Therefore let that abide in you which you heard from the beginning. If what you heard from the beginning abides in you, you also will abide in the Son and in the Father. And this is the promise that He has promised us—eternal life. (1 John 2:24-25)

I was certain that I had eternal life; that became very clear to me.

These things I have written to you who believe in the
name of the Son of God, that you may know that you
have eternal life. (1 John 5:13)

The next thing I realized was that I could never be good enough to
get into heaven on my own merit. As a child, I knew that Jesus loved me,
and because He did, I thought that I might have had something to do
with it. For instance, I thought that I was a pretty good person; after all,
I had never murdered anyone. But my spiritual eyes were opened when
I read in the Bible "Whoever hates his brother is a murderer, and you
know that no murderer has eternal life abiding in him" (1 John 3:15). So
even our thoughts are sin. For instance, if I hate a person, I have already
committed murder. What we think, do, and say will all be judged as sins
of commission. Even things that we don't do that we should do will be
judged—sins of omission.

I realized how sinful I was, and I understood that a believer gets into
heaven because of what Jesus did on the cross. Suddenly, I knew that
Jesus paid the price for the whole human race, not just the nice people.
And I realized that I was not a nice person after all. All of us fall short,
as Romans 3:23 says, "For all have sinned and fall short of the glory of
God." This was something I had never thought of before. Jesus paid the
price for whosoever will come.

For God so loved the world that He gave His only begotten Son,
that whosoever believes in Him should not perish but have everlasting
life. (John 3:16)

Heaven has to be a free gift because none of the human race could
make it. We all miss the mark. In the Greek language, *sin* actually
means "to miss the mark." Only One hit bull's-eye, only One was
without sin, and that is Jesus Christ.

No amount of good works and/or religious deeds will earn me or
anyone a place in heaven. Heaven is a gift from God because He loves.
He knew that we couldn't make it, so He gave the gift of eternal life. It is
free to us but was not free for God. No word in the English language can

aptly describe this act of love. The Greek word *agape* comes the closest. Agape describes sacrifice, action, and love combined. I have heard that it is as the unconditional love that Jesus took to the cross.

Upon hearing these words, I realized that Jesus Christ is Lord—holy and righteous. So I am to be led by Him. I knew then that it was all about Him. He was the leader, not me. He was the fixer of things, not me. He would speak His words through me. He would deal with Terry, not me. He would teach my children through me. I felt like a renewed person. Nothing earthly mattered. It was about Jesus doing what He willed to do in and through me. I knew that life would now be about the Lord and His guiding me. I no longer belonged to myself. I had surrendered. My life was no longer mine:

> Or do you not know that your body is the temple of the Holy Spirit who is in you, whom you have from God, and you are not your own? For you were bought at a price, therefore glorify God in your body and in your spirit, which are God's. (1 Corinthians 6:19–20)

I had been purchased (bought at a price) by Jesus's blood. I hadn't pondered this the way it deserved to be pondered, but now I was learning more. As Matthew 27:50–51a tells us, "Jesus, when He had cried out again with a loud voice, yielded up His Spirit. And behold, the veil of the temple was torn in two from top to bottom ..." The veil was torn in two from top to bottom. What is the significance of the veil being torn? The veil was four inches thick (according to Jewish tradition) and sixty feet high. The size and the thickness make this event even more momentous. Scripture tells us that during Jesus's lifetime, religious life was centered around the holy temple. Animal sacrifices took place there to *cover* the sins of humankind. And once a year, the high priest—and only the high priest—was permitted to pass beyond the veil to enter into God's presence to atone for the sins committed by the people. This day is called the Day of Atonement. This was all according to the law given to Moses by God.

We read in Hebrews 9:3, "And behind the second veil, the part of the tabernacle which is called the Holiest of All …" The Holy of Holies was hidden behind the second veil. This separated man from God. The Holy of Holies was the earthly dwelling place of God's presence. Humankind was separated from a holy God. But when Jesus died on the cross, the veil was torn.

> And behold, the veil of the temple was torn in two from top to bottom; and the earth quaked and the rocks were split, and the graves were opened; and many bodies of the saints who had fallen asleep were raised: and coming out of the graves after His resurrection they went into the holy city and appeared to many. (Matthew 27:51-53)

This, then, is the significance of the veil being torn. Jesus's body on the cross was torn for our sins. His body was torn so that humankind could come boldly to the throne of God. The veil being torn signifies that Jesus paid the price allowing us to enter into the holy of holies. We are now permitted to go into the presence of God.

I felt as if a yoke had been lifted off my shoulders. I felt joy again. My spirit was "quickened"—turned on. My spirit was alive.

> Jesus answered and said to him, "Most assuredly, I say to you, unless one is born again, he cannot see the kingdom of God." Nicodemus said to Him, "How can a man be born when he is old? Can he enter a second time into his mother's womb and be born? Jesus answered, "Most assuredly, I say to you, unless one is born of water and the Spirit, he cannot enter the kingdom of God. That which is born of the flesh is flesh, and that which is born of the Spirit is spirit. (John 3:3–6)

Was I born again—born of the Spirit and not just of flesh?

I thought back to when I was a child. Then, I believed that Jesus died on the cross for my sins, but I hadn't realized how disgusting my sin was or that my sin literally separated me from an all holy God. I knew that I had sinned, but I thought that everyone sinned. I am ashamed to admit that I thought that it was no big deal.

> Teach me Your way O Lord and I will walk in Your truth. (Psalm 86:11)

As a child, I had confessed my sins, but I now realized I had never truly repented. (Remember that *repent* means to change and turn away from your sin.) Now I was truly sorry that I had sinned against an all-holy God. It is the Holy Spirit who convicts us of sin. The Holy Spirit made it very evident to me that I was a broken sinner who needed a Savior. I thought for a moment about the thief on the cross. As a criminal, he asked Jesus if He would remember him when Jesus came into His kingdom.

> Then he said to Jesus, "Lord, remember me when You come into Your kingdom." And Jesus said to him, "Assuredly, I say to you, today you will be with Me in Paradise." (Luke 23:42-43)

Why did Jesus tell the thief that he would be with Jesus today in paradise? Jesus didn't say to the thief, "Get off that cross, and do some good works or spend time in purgatory; then you can come with Me." No, Jesus said he would be with Him that day. The thief believed that Jesus was Lord, and he trusted Jesus alone for eternal life.

We cannot get into heaven with our good works. We cannot do it because heaven is a perfect place, and one sin is one sin too many. God's Word tells us, "You are indeed angry, for we have sinned—in these ways we continue; and we need to be saved. But we are all an unclean thing, and all our righteousness are like filthy rags" (Isaiah 64:5–6). So our good works are as filthy rags to God. God is perfect, and He cannot look upon sin. That is why Jesus came. The thief on the cross believed that Jesus was Lord. That is why Jesus told him that he would be with Him that day. Believing and trusting in Jesus alone for our salvation is the *only* way into perfect heaven.

> For it is by grace you are saved through faith, and that not of yourselves; it is the gift of God, not of works, lest anyone should boast. (Ephesians 2:8-9)

The thief on the cross acknowledged the existence of God. He confessed that he and his companion had transgressed the divine law. He confessed the innocence of Christ and believed in a standard of right and wrong. And he agreed that they were being punished justly, and he confessed that Christ was innocent. I hadn't heard any of this, as I hadn't read the Bible. This was the first time that I heard and understood the gospel. Prior to that point, I hadn't understood what was meant by the *gospel.* I was justified. The word *justified* in the Greek means "to declare righteous."

> being justified freely by His grace through the redemption that is in Christ Jesus, whom God set forth as a propitiation by His blood through faith to demonstrate His righteousness, because in His forbearance God has passed over the sins that were previously committed, to demonstrate at the present time His righteousness, that He might be just and the justifier of the one who has faith in Jesus. (Romans 3:24-26)

This means that God declares a sinner righteous solely on the basis of the merits of Christ's righteousness. So God imputed all believers' sins to Christ's account in His sacrificial death. God imputes Christ's perfect obedience to God's law to Christians. The sinner receives this gift of God's grace by faith alone. And I learned something about that book written on my life—the one filled with all my sin and shame. God's

Word explained that now that I had repented—turned from my sinful ways—and asked Jesus to be my Lord and Savior, the book with all my sin was nailed to the cross with Christ.

> Having wiped out the handwriting of requirements that was against us, which was contrary to us. And He has taken it out of the way, having nailed it to the cross. (Colossians 2:14)

I have been justified as if I had never sinned. If this is not enough, God then sanctifies us daily. Sanctification is the work of God, through which He progressively makes more righteous those whom He has justified. Sanctification always follows justification. We grow in our Christian faith. We read God's Word and obey it. I realized the faith I had as a child was a temporal faith, not a true, saving faith. The term *temporal faith* is used for those who trust in Jesus for all the things needed, things of the world, worldly things. Then they forget and walk away until the next time He is needed. For instance, if I needed a job, I prayed. If I needed help with an exam, I prayed. I was treating Jesus like a cosmic Santa Claus.

I learned that *saving faith* is different. It is a faith that we put in Jesus alone for what He did on the cross to get us into heaven, and we realize there is nothing we can do to help ourselves get in. I had to meditate on this, and when I did, I saw that I must transfer my trust from anything I could do to get into heaven (which is impossible) to what Jesus had already done on the cross. I had a sense of abandonment, trusting in Jesus alone for salvation. I began to understand, and I received this extravagant gift. I understood that this saving faith is the key that opens the door of heaven for me. When the Father sees me, He will see that I am covered by the blood of Jesus.

I have noticed today that some are offended that Jesus went to the cross to shed His blood to save humankind, and they ask why the blood? The answer is this: the shedding of blood is the only way that humankind can be reconciled to the Father. In the Old Testament,

God talks about life being in the blood. Genesis 9:4 says, "But you shall not eat flesh with its life, that is, its blood." Raw blood should not be consumed, as it symbolically represents life. We read in Leviticus 17:11, "For the life of the flesh is in the blood, and I have given it to you upon the altar to make atonement for your souls; for it is the blood that makes atonement for the soul." So it is the blood that atones (make amends) for our souls.

Because blood carries life-sustaining elements to all parts of the body, it represents the essence of life. Pastor and teacher John MacArthur says the following in his commentary: In contrast, the shedding of blood represents the shedding of life, i.e. (Gen.9:4), New Testament references to the shedding of the blood of Jesus Christ are references to His death. Since blood contains the life, blood is sacred to God. Shed blood (death) from a substitute atones for or covers the sinner, who then is allowed to live.

In contrast the blood of animals on the Day of Atonement only covered the sinner's sin and had to be repeated over and over again. But when Jesus died, He died "once for all." The sacrificial work of Christ never needed to be repeated, unlike the Old Testament priestly sacrifices.

> For if the blood of bulls and goats and the ashes of a
> heifer, sprinkling the unclean, sanctifies for the purifying
> of the flesh, how much more shall the blood of Christ,
> Who through the eternal Spirit offered Himself without
> spot to God, cleanse your conscience from dead works,
> to serve the living God? (Hebrews 9:13-14)

I knew from a very young age that Jesus died on the cross for me—the sacrificial death of Jesus—but I am not certain I ever appropriated it for myself. I wasn't fully trusting in Jesus to get me to heaven. I thought I could help myself get in by being a good person (sometimes). I believe that many people today are like I was. This is something that we must ask ourselves: are we trusting fully in what Jesus did on the cross to get us into heaven, or are we trusting partially in ourselves?

As a child, I didn't fully understand atonement—the reconciliation of God and humankind.

> Now then, we are ambassadors for Christ, as though God were pleading through us; we implore you on Christ's behalf, be reconciled to God. For He made Him who knew no sin to be sin for us, that we might become the righteousness of God in Him. (2 Corinthians 5:20–21)

> Jesus paid my debt and yours so that we would be reconciled to God. The unfair exchange. It was Luther that prayed: "Oh, Lord Jesus, Thou art my righteousness – I am Thy sin!" I am so grateful for this, are you?

> Today we still don't fully understand atonement. I have heard that there are four biblical views of the atonement. There are questions like, "Did Jesus have to die?" He did, just read His prayer to the Father when He was sweating drops of blood (the medical term is *hematidrosis*) in the garden of Gethsemane (Luke 22:44); there was no other way. Also, a score had to be settled for the sins of the human race, and Jesus was the only sinless One who could accomplish this. When Jesus died on the cross, He defeated the devil by conquering death for those who will believe. Remember He died for "whosoever, will come" (John 3:16).

As always, C. S. Lewis said something very simple, yet profound of the atonement: He said, "We don't have to understand it for it to work." In the Old Testament, Adam and Eve were sent out of the garden of Eden because in it stood the tree of life. Once they had sinned and eaten from the tree of the knowledge of good and evil in Genesis 2:16–17, God, in His mercy, made sure that they couldn't eat from the tree of life; if they had, they (we) would have lived forever (Genesis 3:22, 24) in a fallen, sinful state. Instead, the plan was stated in Genesis 3:15—God Gave His only begotten Son to pay the debt of humankind.

As a child, I knew that Jesus died for my sins, and I was so very thankful. But I wasn't aware that I should surrender all I am to Jesus and trust Him alone to direct my life.

> Trust in the Lord with all your heart, and lean not on your own understanding; but in all your ways acknowledge Him, and He shall direct your paths. (Proverbs 3:5–6)

Up until this point, I had never let Jesus rule my life. I was ignorant of the fact that my Lord should direct my steps; I'd always done it all myself. This day was different; this day I made Jesus Lord of my life. I slipped off the imaginary throne in my heart and asked Jesus to sit on it and direct my life from that day onward. I didn't worry about my job anymore because I knew that the Lord would take care of it. I knew this was the same Jesus who was in my bedroom as a child. He was saying to me, "I am bringing you back to that little girl that I created."

> But the anointing which you have received from Him abides in you …
> (1 John 2:27a)

It was as if Jesus was saying, "I created you to love people, to be the peacemaker, not an antagonist; to build people up, not tear them down." Did this mean that Jesus would erase the last twenty years and continue from where He left off *before* my father died and all the other tragedies occurred? Before I turned my back on Jesus and did everything my way?

> So great is His mercy towards those who fear Him; As far as the east is from the west, So far has He removed our transgressions from us.
> (Psalm 103:11–12)

9

Chapter

FORGIVEN / NEW LIFE

I WAS TOTALLY FORGIVEN; the chains were broken. I was completely free.

> Now the Lord is the Spirit; and where the Spirit of the Lord is, there is liberty. But we all, with unveiled face, beholding as in a mirror the glory of the Lord, are being transformed into the same image from glory to glory, just as by the Spirit of the Lord. (2 Corinthians 3:17-18)

My debt had been paid in full. Jesus left His heavenly home to save all of us, including me, from sin and death. This extravagant, unconditional, sacrificial love brought God to earth to pay for our sins. Jesus paid on the cross for every sin that was ever committed. Will you receive it? Love put and kept Him on that cross. He died, but three days later, He rose again. Jesus said in Matthew 20:18–19, "Behold, we are going up to Jerusalem, and the Son of Man will be betrayed to the chief priests and to the scribes, and they will condemn Him to death, and deliver Him to the Gentiles to mock and to scourge and to crucify. And the third day He will rise again."

Death could not hold Him.

But the angel answered and said to the women, "Do not be afraid, for I know that you seek Jesus who was crucified. He is not here; for He is risen, as He said. Come see the place where the Lord lay." (Matthew 28:5–6)

Jesus rose from the dead, as He said.

For I delivered to you first of all that which I also received: that Christ died for our sins according to the Scriptures, and that He was buried, and that He rose again the third day according to the Scriptures, and that He was seen by Cephas, then by the twelve. After that He was seen by other five hundred brethren at once, of whom the greater part remain to the present, but some have fallen asleep. (1 Corinthians 15:3–6)

At the young age of three, I heard and believed that Jesus died for me. And I heard that He rose again after three days. But I hadn't realized this was an unfair exchange. His righteousness imputed to me, while Jesus, the perfect sacrifice, took my filthy sin upon Himself.

For He made Him who knew no sin to be sin for us, that we might become the righteousness of, God in Him. (2 Corinthians 5:21)

Jesus has paid the price so His purpose could be accomplished through His people. He uses those who seek Him. Those who seek Him will find Him.

Ask and it will be given; seek and you will find; knock and it will be open to you. (Matthew 7:7)

How ironic that the job that I was so intimidated by actually led me back to life. But Jesus knew what it would take to get me back. He is the Master builder.

> Unless the Lord builds the house, they labor in vain who build it. (Psalm 127:1)

The Lord would begin to rebuild my house. Incidentally, the Lord kept me at this company for ten and a half years. Through all the ups and downs, I became one of their top producers nationwide. Why? Because I wasn't doing the driving anymore. I had moved into the passenger seat and let Jesus drive. He, being perfect, does all things perfectly and for our good. The Lord continued to change me from the inside out. He knows all things (omniscient) and knew that I would need a manual to live life with Him properly. He arranged for this to happen.

A couple of months earlier, when I interviewed for this job, I met Sharon, a lovely lady who is still my dear friend today. She was the secretary to the managers. She mentioned that she went to a church in Costa Mesa called Calvary Chapel. I remembered that the pastor that I had been listening to on the radio was from Calvary Chapel Riverside. Sharon asked me if I had a Bible; I told her no. The next time I saw her, she handed me a Bible—a "one-year" Bible. This Bible affords the reader to read the entire sixty-six books in just one year. At thirty-five years of age, I began to read the Bible for the first time in my life.

> For the word of God is living and powerful, and sharper than any two-edged sword, piercing even to the division of soul and spirit, and of joints and marrow, and is a discerner of the thoughts and intents of the heart. (Hebrews 4:12)

I now had a manual to live by, to do it God's way instead of my way. I learned that the Word of God is so vital to a Christian's life. David said in Psalm 138:2c, "For You have Magnified Your Word above all Your name."

He esteems His word above His name?

But the Word of the Lord endures forever. (1 Peter 1:25)

So the Word of God is eternal?

God immediately started to work in my life. Through reading God's Word, I learned that His Word is able to save our souls.

> Therefore lay aside all filthiness and overflow of wickedness, and receive with meekness the implanted Word which is able to save your souls. (James 1:21)

I fell totally in love with Jesus. I was more joyful and less sad. The anger I had carried since my father's death was gone because I had an understanding. My earthly father was not my heavenly Father.

> A Father of the fatherless, a defender of widows, is God in His Holy habitation. God sets the solitary in families; He brings out those who are bound into prosperity; But the rebellious dwell in a dry land. (Psalm 68:5-6)

I had wandered into a very dry land, but I'd found my oasis. I was being watered and washed by the Word of God. I continued to listen to the radio every day. At times I would turn the Christian radio off or listen to something else, only to turn it back again. I had become hungry for God's Word.

I would listen to a program in which the hosts would answer questions and counter the cults. A cult would be described as a group that does not believe that Jesus Christ came in the flesh. Fully God, yet fully Man. Evidence would be given from the Bible on Who Jesus is. I was particularly interested in this kind of reasoning known as Apologetics. *Apologia* in Greek means defense.

> But sanctify the Lord God in your hearts, and always be ready to give a defense (apologia) to everyone who asks you a reason for the hope that is in you, with meekness and fear. (1 Peter 3:15)

I heard different parts of the gospel, time and time again. The radio preachers became my professors on air. I learned quite a lot quickly.

It is the Word of God that brings life. I pondered that for a while. I never had the Word of God. I had missed it. So if Jesus is the Word of God, then had I missed Jesus? I thought that I knew Jesus. I thought that I loved Him. I didn't know that *the Word* was one of the names for Jesus.

> In the beginning was the Word, the Word was with God the Word was God. (John 1:1)

The Word was God. Two primary Greek words that describe Scripture are translated as "word" in the New Testament. One word is *rhema*, and it literally means utterance, which means the spoken word. Rhema signifies the action of utterance. The second word is *logos*, which describes the inspired Word of God.

> All scripture is given by inspiration of God, and is profitable for doctrine, for reproof, for correctness, for instruction in righteousness, that the man of God may be complete, thoroughly equipped for every good work. (2 Timothy 3:16)

So the Word of God became flesh and dwelt among us. This is what the Bible says in John 1:14, "And the Word became flesh and dwelt among us, and we beheld His glory." Yes, Jesus is Fully God and Fully Man. I believed that Jesus was God incarnate. So God became flesh.

> By this you will know the Spirit of God: Every spirit that
> confesses that Jesus Christ came in the flesh is of God,
> and every spirit that does not confess that Jesus Christ
> came in the flesh is not of God. And this is the spirit of
> the antichrist ... (1 John 4:2-3)

I meditated on this for some time, so much so that I learned about this paradox that changed the world. After two thousand years, we still worship Him. The calendar was changed because of Him. People are changed when they receive Him. The paradox is that God became Man, commonly known as the incarnation, 100 percent God and 100 percent Man—not 50/50.

Another term used in Christian circles is the *hypostatic union*. This term hypostatic is derived from the Greek word *hypostasis*, meaning personal. Hence, the hypostatic union means "the personal union" or the joining of the two natures of Jesus—His divine and human natures. The nature of something includes all its qualities or attributes. Jesus retained all of His divine attributes; He remained Fully God. But He set His deity aside and became Fully Human in order to reconcile God and humankind.

> Now all things are of God, who has reconciled us to
> Himself through Jesus Christ, and has given us the
> ministry of reconciliation, that is, that God was in Christ
> reconciling the world to Himself ... (2 Corinthians
> 5:18–19)

Christ became Man to save man. He humbled Himself and became one of us.

> Who being in the form of God, did not consider it
> robbery to be equal with God, but made Himself of
> no reputation, taking the form of a bondservant, and
> coming in the likeness of men. And being found in

appearance as a man He humbled Himself and became obedient to the point of death, even the death of the cross. (Philippians 2:6, 8)

Looking further into God becoming Man, I came across a book by Dr. Michael Guillen, a former Harvard physics instructor, called *Amazing Truths*. In every chapter, Dr. Guillen states some amazing truths. Although I am not so knowledgeable in the sciences, I found this book fascinating and pored over certain chapters a number of times, including chapter 5, "Not of This World." Dr. Guillen writes about light and the speed of light. He quotes scripture at the beginning of every chapter. In chapter 5, he uses 1 John 1:5—"God is light; in Him there is no darkness at all." He speaks of a discovery made by Einstein, in which matter and energy are interchangeable—matter and energy, once thought to be as disparate as apples and oranges, are, in fact, interchangeable. He quotes Einstein's own words: "Mass and Energy are both but different manifestations of the same thing." Michael Guillen, *Amazing Truths* (Grand Rapids, MI, Zondervan, 2015), page number(s) 70,75.

In his book, Guillen gives his interpretation (in plain English) of a quote from Einstein on the speed of light, stating "the speed of light is, in a very real sense of the word, sacred." Guillen, *Amazing*, page number(s) 73,75. He writes that human beings can become light, but we need to die first for our bodies to be converted completely into pure human energy. I thought of John 12:23–24, which tells us, "But Jesus answered them saying, 'The hour has come that the Son of Man should be glorified. Most assuredly I say to you, unless a grain of wheat falls to the ground and dies, it remains alone; but if it dies it produces much grain.'"

Guillen said that "the opposite can happen too, for instance light can be transformed into ordinary matter—like flesh and blood. Guillen said that "these two possibilities are not merely theoretical. Today these processes are known as 'pair annihilation' and 'pair creation." He states that in the Bible, God and Jesus are repeatedly identified with light. He goes on to say, "Scripture states the equivalence so emphatically, 'God is light in Him is no darkness at all' (1 John 1:5)—that I have long since concluded it represents not just a pretty metaphor, but an amazing truth worthy of serious contemplation. A truth remarkably in line with our modern scientific understanding of light." Guillen. *Amazing*, page number(s) 75,76. This is something that I have not looked into properly yet, but I do know that Jesus is always associated with light. John 8:12 tells us, "I am the light of the world ..."

John MacArthur speaks about this same verse in his Bible commentary while speaking on Hebrews 1:3 "Who being the brightness of His glory and the express image of His person ..." MacArthur teaches on brightness. He says, "The term is used only here in the NT. It expresses the concept of sending forth light or shining as in John 8:12." He goes on to say "that the meaning of the word 'brightness' must not be mistaken with the word reflection. The Son is not just reflecting God's glory; He is God and radiates His own essential glory." John MacArthur, *The MacArthur Bible Commentary*, (Nashville, TN. Thomas Nelson, 2005) pages 1835,36. I do know that Scripture speaks of not needing any light in heaven because Jesus is the light.

> The city had no need of the sun or the moon in it, for the glory of God illuminated it, The Lamb is its light. (Revelation 21:23)

Dr. Guillen states,

> Science has done a fabulous job of helping elucidate the critical importance of sunshine to us and our planet. Deprived of sunshine, plants will wither and die-along with all the animals sustained by them. Deprived of sunshine, we can become depressed as well. The affliction is called SAD—seasonal affective disorder— and psychologists treat it primarily with large doses of light.

Guillen, *Amazing*, page number(s) 80,81.

To me this translates to large doses of Jesus.

> And this is the condemnation, that the light as come
> into the world, and men loved darkness rather than
> light, because their deeds were evil ... (John 3:19)

Genesis 1:3 says, "Let there be light." Are we to be light? I think that the apostle Paul would say yes. Ephesians 5:8 tells us, "You were once darkness, but now you are light in the Lord. Live as children of light." Without this act of God reconciling the human race to Him through His Son, we would get what we deserve—hell. But because our God is a God of love, He gave His only begotten Son to be the Savior for humankind.

Further in my random studies, I took a look at the Holy Trinity—Father, Son, and Holy Spirit. The word trinity, dissected, is *tri*, equaling three, and *unity*, equaling one—three in one. One God, three coeternal, consubstantial (being of the same essence) persons. One essence; three coeternal persons. So Jesus is the same essence as the Father.

Jesus said in John 10:30, "I and the Father are one." When Philip asked Jesus, in John 14:8, "Lord show us the Father, and it is sufficient for us," Jesus said to him, "Have I been with you so long, and yet you have not known Me, Philip? He who has seen Me has seen the Father ..." Jesus and the Father are one essence. Jesus was God's perfect revelation of Himself. C. S. Lewis wrote that God begets God. It makes sense. Cat begets cat, and dog begets dog, so God begets God—an intimate, relational triune God; the One true God.

> Hear O Israel, the Lord our God is One ...
> (Deuteronomy 6:4)

The Hebrew word for *one* is *echad*. It means unity, not singularity. It is also used in Genesis 2:24, referring to a husband and wife becoming one. The Hebrew word to describe singular is *yachid*, and it is never used in the Hebrew scripture in reference to God; only echad is used. We also see in Genesis 1:26 that God says, "Let Us make man in Our image."

I read an article that explained a little about the names of God. I read that in the Biblical Hebrew in Genesis 1:1, "In the beginning God," the name used for God is Elohim, so it's "In the beginning Elohim." I learned that the noun Elohim is *plural* but always used with a *singular* verb when speaking of the true God. This again indicates a unity and a diversity within the nature of God. In scripture, this unity and diversity is revealed in the doctrine of the Trinity.

Elohim can also be used as false gods (Exodus 20:33) and angels (Psalm 8:6) and refers to humans in Psalm 82:6, probably referring to judges and/or magistrates. The singular *El* has an idea of strength, power, and might. Elohim is the general name for God and is used in the context of God as Creator. Yahweh (the Lord) is God's personal name and is used in the context of God having a relationship with His people.

In the Old and New Testaments, many Scriptures help us to understand who God is. The Trinity may be a difficult concept to grasp, yet we see the concept in God's Word. In the New Testament, some of the Scriptures indicating the Trinity are: Colossians 1:16-17, 2:9; John 14:8; John 1:14; John 10:30; and Luke 1:35. Jesus's baptism in Matthew 3:16–17 is another indication of the Trinity. Also, Jesus said, "Go, therefore and make disciples of all nations, baptizing them in the Name of the Father and of the Son and of the Holy Spirit" (Matthew 28:19). When He spoke the word *name*, He used it in a singular sense.

For me, it is 1x1x1=1. This loving God is all-knowing (omniscient). He knew that Adam and Eve would fall. We are born in the original sin of Adam and Eve, in corruption. But Jesus is the incorruptible seed. We see this in Genesis 3:15, which says, "And I will put enmity between you and the woman, and between your seed and her Seed; He shall bruise your head, and you shall bruise His heel." When I heard John MacArthur explain this passage, I understood that God ultimately cursed Satan. The struggle is between "your seed" (Satan and unbelievers who are called the devil's children in John 8:44) and "her Seed" (Christ, a descendant of Eve and those in Him). John MacArthur, *MacArthur commentary*, page(s) 17.

In the book of Romans, Paul encourages the believers in Rome, as he says, "And the God of peace will crush Satan under your feet shortly" (Romans 16:20). There was much to learn. I had to meditate on God's Word. The Word is life. It is truth. It is God-breathed and, I believe, inerrant.

10

Chapter

ALIVE IN THE SPIRIT

I BEGAN TO REALLY live (born of the Spirit, not only flesh) in 1986 at the age of thirty-five. I found the identity in Jesus that I had been searching for.

> For in Him dwells all the fullness of the God-head
> bodily; and you are complete in Him ... (Colossians 2:9)

I am complete in Jesus, and just as Jesus says, "I have come that you may have life, and that they may have it more abundantly" (John 10:10b). I would live life more abundantly. I would love those who are still living outside of the family of God. I would go and give the truth of the gospel to all peoples. I would show Jesus's love to those in prison, to those in the gay community, allowing Jesus's true love to pour over them through me. I must begin to die to self. It couldn't be my love, only the pure Love of Jesus flowing through me.

> And above all things have fervent love for one another,
> for "love will cover a multitude of sins." (1 Peter 4:8)

I would keep in mind and communicate that their sins are no greater than my own, and vice versa. I would explain repentance (to turn from sin and not do it again; leave it behind). I'm reminded of when Jesus spoke to the woman caught in adultery. What did He say?

> "Woman, where are those accusers of yours Has no one condemned you?" She said, "No one, Lord." And Jesus said to her, "Neither do I condemn you; go and sin no more." (John 8:1, 12)

So Jesus told the woman that He did not condemn her, but He did say "Go and sin no more" Jesus is the light of the world, and if we follow Him, we will have the light of life.

> I am the light of the world. He who follows Me shall not walk in darkness, but have the light of life. (John 8:12)

Jesus is my arbiter. What He says, I will do. I also would visit the widows and widowers in their loneliness. My family would also benefit. James and Daniel were just turning six, and Angela had just turned two when the Lord began to use me. He opened my mouth, and it became very clear to me that I was to tell people about Jesus.

> Now therefore, go, and I will be with your mouth and teach you what you shall say. (Exodus 4:12)

Well, of course this was it! I thought back over my life, to those times when I felt that I had something to tell someone—someone like my dad before he died; someone like Micky before he vanished from this world; someone like my brother Jimmy before he made that terrible mistake and took his own life; someone like little Valerie before she was so brutally murdered. Now I knew what I had to do. I had to tell others about who Jesus is and what He did for them. I had to give them the truth of the gospel.

I had a pang of sorrow in my heart as I thought of all those people I had met prior to this time. They all needed a Savior, yet I hadn't told them. From now on, it would be different. I remembered that wooden picture in my bedroom. At times I had asked if the Lord would open that door, and then there were times when I wanted it to be kept shut. But I had it all wrong. The artist had left the handle off the door intentionally. The door represents our hearts, and the handle is on the inside. I mistakenly thought Jesus had to open that door, but Jesus is knocking on the door of our hearts. We must open the door and let Him in.

> Behold, I stand at the door and knock. If anyone hears
> My voice and opens the door, I will come in and dine
> with him and he with Me. (Revelation 3:20)

I was still quite a novice, but I was so alive in the Spirit. Like it or not, my job was to *tell*. In the grocery store, I heard two young girls using Jesus's name as a curse word. I walked up to them and told them that I could not bear to hear Jesus's name being used like that. I told them who He was and what He had done for them. They seemed stunned. Now they had something to consider. It didn't matter where I was; the Spirit of God opened my mouth to begin a spiritual conversation. My heart became tender toward the elderly in convalescent and nursing homes. I often thought of those without family. It was as if the Lord was asking me to visit those who sat in their rooms, waiting for someone— anyone—to come.

Could any of them remember what touch felt like? I sought out the nearest nursing homes and took my children with me. Over a year or so, my children saw firsthand what Jesus does when a person understands that they have been bought at a price, this life for His use. As the children got busy with their sports, I would go alone. I had been visiting Virgil, who much older than ninety when he passed and a Christian. As Virgil was moved to different nursing homes, I would follow him as one of his friends and visitors. This allowed me to talk with other elderly people about Jesus.

I always visited on a Saturday afternoon. On one such day, Virgil was asleep, so I talked with Louie in the next bed. Louie was a wonderful

Jewish man who didn't mind my speaking to him about Jesus. The Lord gave me favor with Louie. He would sing Jewish songs to me. My heart longed for him to know Jesus as the true Messiah, so I continued to tell him. He listened.

The man in the third bed by the door beckoned me to come over and help him. I knew that I shouldn't help any of the patients; rather, I should call the nurse. I did that. Standing by the open door, I called for assistance. Nurses were scurrying back and forth but none came our way. I felt in my spirit that the Lord was warning me not to go near him. I thought I was sensing that there were three unclean spirits in this man. But the man continued to beckon me. He had his index finger caught in the top of his gown. I moved over to him. His expression was almost sneering. These words ran through my mind: *You are ugly, but Jesus loves you.*

As I went to release his finger, he pulled back his fist and, with full force, hit me on the bridge of my nose, which bled. I took a quick step or two back and looked back at him. His eyes were evil. I decided to tell the nurse on the way out, and she replied, "Oh, he does that sometimes." Well, that was a lesson for me to learn. I had sensed the Lord telling me not to go but I went anyway. It was time to be more careful.

> If any of you lacks wisdom, let him ask of God, who
> gives to all liberally and without reproach ... (James 1:5)

Every time I went back in that room, I wore my crucifix at the back of me, so it faced that man in the third bed by the door.

We were planning another trip to London to visit family. On our last trip, I had tried to indoctrinate my sisters and friends with the lie of astrology. It was my topic of conversation. This time would be different. It was clear to my heart that the Lord was imparting instruction to me.

> See then that you walk circumspectly, not as fools but
> as wise, redeeming the time, because the days are evil.
> Therefore do not be unwise, but understand what the

will of the Lord is. And do not be drunk with wine, in
which is dissipation; but be filled with the Spirit ...
(Ephesians 5:15, 18)

The Lord seemed to be speaking to my heart, saying; "From now
on, you will be speaking My name. If you drink alcohol, you will slur
My name." Although not big drinkers, my family would have beer and
wine at all their functions. Without any judgment on any of my family
or fellow Christians who have the liberty in the Lord to drink alcohol,
I was now to decline. I wasn't the same person.

Come out from among them and be separate, says the
Lord. (2 Corinthians 6:17)

I had to tell them that I was very wrong to promote astrology. I
made it clear that astrology is idolatry, and 1 Corinthians 10:14 says,
"Therefore my beloved, flee from idolatry." We are to consult the Lord,
not the stars that He created.

Then God said, "Let there be lights in the firmament
of the heavens to divide the day from the night...and let
them be for lights in the firmament of the heavens to
give light on the earth; and it was so. (Genesis 1:14-15)

Astrology is not something to dwell on or live by, as I had a tendency
to do. Instead, God is to be worshipped as the Creator of the universe
and all that is within it.

To whom then will you liken Me, or whom shall I be
equal? Says the Holy One. Lift up your eyes on high,
and see who has created these things, who brings out
their hosts by number, He calls them all by name, by the
greatness of His might and the strength of His power;
not one is missing. (Isaiah 40:25, 26)

While I was there, I tried to teach my sisters everything I had been learning. They listened. My nephews and nieces mocked me, but they were young.

> Then I said, "I will not make mention of Him, nor speak anymore in His name." But His Word was like a burning fire shut up in my bones; I was weary of holding back, and I could not. For I heard many mocking... (Jeremiah 20:9–10)

My sisters, who knew Jesus in the way I had, were happy to ask Jesus to be their Lord and Savior. But they were not getting the teaching that I was. I don't believe they were seeking Him the way I was being called to do.

> And don't be conformed to this world, but be transformed by the renewing of your mind, that you may prove what is that good and acceptable and perfect will of God. (Romans 12:2)

Before I became born again, I enjoyed all what the world had to offer. But now, in certain places, I felt like a fish out of water.

> And you He made alive, who were dead in trespasses and sins in which you once walked according to the course of this world, according to the prince of the power of the air ... (Ephesians 2:1-2)

To make matters worse, Terry was still the same person. He enjoyed all the same things, which is quite understandable. He was not under God's grace yet. I felt alone. But how could I say that because I had Jesus, who meant everything to me. My mother didn't quite understand me either. She thought that Jesus wouldn't like it if I was to talk to people about Him. She thought that religion should be kept undercover. One of my sisters made a similar remark. I answered her with part of the following scripture:

> You are the light of the world. A city that is set on a hill
> cannot be hidden. Nor can they light a lamp and put
> it under a basket, but on a high lampstand, and it gives
> light to all who are in the house. (Matthew 5:14–15)

Back in the States, my coworkers knew that I was a Christian. My job was tough. I was learning how to hand it over to the Lord instead of doing it in my own strength. I always had the desire to meet and exceed my annual sales plan. If we exceeded the plan by 20 percent, we won a trip to places like Spain, Ireland, Bermuda. It seemed I won every other year. That wasn't good enough for me; I wanted to win most years. It wasn't because I wanted to go on the trips because that seemed rather shallow to me. But there was still a lot of self in me, and I strived to win (all is vanity). So my flesh was warring against the Spirit.

> For the flesh lusts against the Spirit, and the Spirit against
> the flesh: and these are contrary to one another, so that
> you do not do the things that you wish. (Galatians 5:17)

I was in love with my Lord, and it had become hard for me to live in a world so full of unimportant entertainment. Yet I still was striving in the flesh. At home, Terry and I were doing the best we could to be a family. We were always with the children. Terry wasn't drinking much or buying pot. Parties had ceased. However, now we were unequally yoked.

> Do not be unequally yoked together with unbelievers. For
> what fellowship has righteousness with lawlessness? …
> (2 Corinthians 6:14)

I didn't dwell on what we didn't have. I knew that I had a job to do, and God gave me tunnel vision. Whether I spoke with neighbors, parents from the children's sports teams, people in grocery stores, passersby, or the cults (who stopped knocking after a few conversations), I had a joy about me that made it all worthwhile. The odd thing is I never presented the gospel to Terry. That was partly because I hadn't learned a way to give it—I didn't know where to start—and partly because I thought that he would get annoyed at me and shut me down.

My children were my main concern. I prayed and asked Jesus to help me teach them about Him. I prayed that they would know Him and He them. He created them in His image for good works. I gave them each a Psalm, and later, I wrote the words of a Dylan song that has profound words, "Forever Young." I thought it was quite evident that Angela had faith in Jesus. She would write beautiful notes to her dad and me (I still have most of them), speaking of how Jesus was always with us and that He loved us. I thought if Terry would listen to anyone at this time, it might be Angela.

Out of the mouth of babes … (Psalm 8:2)

James and Daniel knew Jesus. Daniel was a "seer," and James was full of loyal, quiet wisdom. They were wonderfully active boys. A nun once told me that one of them would become a priest.

But you are a chosen generation a royal priesthood …
(1 Peter 2:9)

Daniel sees in the Spirit, bypassing the natural. Now he ministers to people who are in the hospital, praying for a healing in Jesus's name. He takes the whole family with him. James is a wonderful friend, a compassionate believer, and is always helping someone somewhere. He's someone that one can rely on. They both have much discernment. Angela is a warrior for Christ. She speaks the Word, believing that the Word is the only truth. She has the gift of discernment.

When they were young, it wasn't easy having them read the Bible. Often, I would sit in a room with them adamant about teaching them Scripture, with one boy jumping on the bed, one under it, and Angela drawing or writing. But I would not give up. I purchased tapes from the pastor in Riverside, and at night I put James and Daniel to bed listening to his preaching.

> My Word never comes back void but accomplishes what I send it to do. (Isaiah 55:11)

> Today, all our children read the Bible. Do not give up with teaching your children about the love of the Father, Son, and Holy Spirit. The Lord is all powerful and all knowing, and He will honor your teaching of His Word.

The nun was right, but it isn't just one of my boys. I know that all of my children are priests, according to God's Word.

> But you are a chosen generation, a royal priesthood, a holy nation, His own special people, that you may proclaim the praises of Him who called you out of the darkness into His marvelous light. (1 Peter 2:9)

Oh yes, what a marvelous light we have in Jesus, our Lord and our God. And all of you who believe and cling to and trust in Jesus for eternal life can claim this same Scripture together with us.

11
Chapter

OUT OF THE MOUTH OF BABES (PSALM 8:2)

I T WAS AROUND 1990 when Angela said she didn't like the church we were attending. I knew why. She wasn't being taught from the Bible. I was involved in teaching the children. And I took every opportunity to use Scripture in my teaching. I was also a part of a confidential ministry that encouraged women who needed a friend. But I was feeling the same as Angela, and now, fully aware that the Word of God is living and powerful and sharper than any two-edged sword, I wanted the children to be at a Bible-teaching church. I had been praying, asking Jesus to show me where He wanted us. My heart was set on Calvary Chapel, but the nearest was Riverside. It would mean that we would travel for over an hour to get there. I opted for the next best thing—a Bible-teaching church close by. They had an evangelism program about to begin.

> And He Himself gave some to the apostles, some prophets, some evangelists and some pastors and teachers, for the equipping of the saints for the work of the ministry, for the edifying of the body of Christ ... (Ephesians 4:11-12)

The evangelism group was small. There are many ways to give the truth of the gospel but only one gospel. This one began with two provocative questions that, when answered, gave a pretty good idea of where the person was spiritually. I had some studying to do.

> Be diligent to present yourselves approved to God, a worker who does not need to be ashamed, rightly dividing the Word of truth. (2 Timothy 2:15)

I loved it and knew that this was where the Lord wanted me. When I was out on the street, talking to someone about Jesus, I knew that I was in the right place, in my element. Proverbs 11:30 says, "He who wins souls is wise." I now could see that the Lord had been training me over the years, putting me through all of those tough sales jobs just to bring me to a place where I would fulfill His purpose. I was privileged to do the Lord's bidding.

> For we are not, as so many, peddling the Word of God; but as of sincerity, but as from God, we speak in the sight of God in Christ. (2 Corinthians 2:17)

We met at a small church, where we would pray and then venture out into the streets or go to people who might have visited the church but hadn't returned. We asked the Lord to send us His divine appointments, asking if He would give the gospel through us. He did.

> You shall speak My words to them whether they hear or whether they refuse ...
> (Ezekiel 2:7)

We see many souls come to Christ.

> I planted, Apollos watered, but God gave the increase.
> (1 Corinthians 3:6)

It is the Holy Spirit's power (dunamis power,) speaking through His willing vessels.

> For we do not preach ourselves, but Christ Jesus the Lord, and ourselves your bondservants for Jesus sake. (2 Corinthians 4:5)

I was a bondservant of Christ's, and still working my tough sales job. The Lord had used it to strengthen me and also to show me the many flaws in my personality.

> Be strong and of good courage do not fear nor be afraid of them for the Lord your God He is the One who goes before you. He will not leave you nor forsake you. (Deuteronomy 31:6)

But now it looked like it was time for a change. I hadn't been looking for another job, but one afternoon I received a phone call from a former associate and friend. She said she'd been working for an international company in the recruitment industry, and she remembered that this had been my line of work. This company was looking for a senior account executive to work in an office that was near where I lived.

I got the job, and in July 1996, I began working again in the industry that I loved—the people industry. My office was four miles from my house. This was a very busy office. The manager was a woman, and six other women also worked there. I was happy, but there was one very big wrinkle. All my working life I had managed my own business the way I chose from beginning to end. I was the one interviewing the people, and I was the one to place them in the job. I did it all. It was as if whoever I was helping was my responsibility. Well, this company had a different philosophy, and I had to learn how to be (fully) part of a team. I didn't realize how difficult it would be, and the Lord showed me that I must hold very lightly to everything in this world and let it go. I needed to trust in Him alone for all results.

> But seek first the kingdom of God and His righteousness,
> and all these things shall be added to you. (Matthew
> 6:33)

My responsibility was to secure job vacancies in order to put a temporary employee to work. I would then hand the open job order over to the recruitment office, who would then place a person in the job opening. I had no say whatsoever on who would be placed into the position. It took me a few weeks, but I was good-humored about it, knowing that the Lord knew best. In my soul I felt that the Lord was telling me that this was where He wanted me because it was better and necessary for me. He was taking care of me as He always had.

> Therefore humble yourselves under the mighty hand of
> God, that He may exalt you in due time, casting your
> cares upon Him, for He cares for you.
> (1 Peter 5:6-7)

I was as happy as one could be in a job. After a while, I noticed that all of the wonderful relationships that I was building were predominately with women. I asked the Lord if He wanted me to start something like a women's group, and because it's not the Lord's way to plainly tell us what He would have us do, I took a step of faith. If it flew, then it was good, but if it failed, I would back off. This was my way of knowing what the Lord wanted me to do.

A wonderful Christian business associate (a woman who was miraculously healed of an aggressive cancer) and I started a women's breakfast group. After a few weeks of praying, we realized that this was not what the Lord had in mind. I patiently continued working, believing there was a reason for these great business relationships.

Life seemed easier, or maybe it was because I trusted in the Lord alone and knew that He would accomplish, in His time, what He purposed for my life. My children were growing; the boys were eighteen, and Angela was fourteen years old. Terry seemed quite happy. His mother had moved from Pennsylvania to live near us. She wouldn't live with us because she said if she did, Terry and I would probably divorce due to another person's opinion. She was wise. She lived in a very nice senior apartment a few streets from us. We took her everywhere we went. I always enjoyed being with her. She had a good sense of humor, like Terry, but she was more ornery than he was.

The reason I loved her most was because she loved Jesus. We could talk all day about the Lord. When we went out to eat, which was often, Terry would get annoyed and say, "Can you two talk about anything other than Jesus?" We would both laugh and say no. We both knew our Bible to some degree and loved discussing His Word.

Life at home had become a challenge. The worst thing that can happen to a mother is that her children run wild. The boys got into the party scene. They were drinking more than just on the weekends. On one occasion, the ladies at my work used them in a temporary position. One of them was sent home because he was still intoxicated from the previous night. For me, this posed a major problem, as I'd grown up watching my dad go from man to mouse. I knew all too well that my sons were falling for the devil's lie.

But my faith was strong, and although I hadn't learned to speak over my children with God's Word, I prayed and believed that my God was faithful and would bring them back to Him. But how long would that take? My life was consumed with prayer for all three of my children. Each time I came in contact with a Christian, I would ask that person to pray with me for James, Daniel, and Angela. I would never hesitate because I knew that the Lord heard and saw everything. When Angela and I went to Corona Del Mar, to get baptized, I came up out of the water and asked Pastor Chuck to please pray for them. Pastor Chuck said, in his wonderful, resounding voice, "James and Daniel," as if those names dripped slowly with Holy Spirit oil into his heart.

The effective fervent prayer of a righteous man avails
much … (James 5:16)

Days and nights both were long. There is very little sleep at night
for a mother who is waiting for the kids to come home. We did have
curfews but not enough follow-through on my and Terry's part. On
one occasion, Terry had left for work, and a policeman knocked on
my door about 4:30 a.m. and said, "I have your son in the car." I asked
which one, he told me and continued to say that he should impound
my son's truck, which would cost a lot of money to get out again. Then
he looked at me and said, "But you know, there is something about this
kid. I believe that he is really a good kid, and what happened tonight
may have taught him a lesson." He explained that he had told my son
that he may have to go to court.

Apparently, my son had made a U-turn at a convenience store, and
the officer spotted him. The officer checked him for intoxication and
determined he was driving under the influence. This police officer
seemed kind and even spiritual, so I asked, "Are you a Christian?" When
he said that he was, I then asked him what he thought the Lord would
have us do.

He replied, "I have put your son through a lot tonight. I'll call
him in."

In the house, he came, sobbing and muttering something about
moving away from all his friends. The officer and I told him that he
could not blame this on friends and that he must take full responsibility
for his actions. The officer finally left; I was so thankful for him. I knew
that the Lord was with us by sending this particular police officer to my
door. I begged the Lord to make Himself known to my sons.

My other son also got into a similar situation later that year and
ended up in a detention center. He and a friend had been caught
drinking liquor at a local mall and had a run-in with the security guard.
When my son called me from the detention center, he begged me to
come for him, saying, "They're going to send me to jail if you don't
respond, Mom."

I asked him, "Why should I make it easy for you?" I held back for as long as I could, again imploring the Lord for wisdom to know what He would have me do. I wanted my son to reconsider his actions. Shortly before he was to go to jail, I called and had him released. These two incidences seemed to have taught them both a lesson. They finally stopped the partying at age twenty or so.

Thank You, Lord, for keeping them through it all. Use them now for Your glory, Lord.

Angela, whom I would have trusted with my life, was living life and watching all of this. She didn't say much, but there was so much more than meets the eye. A decision she was to make would be devastatingly hard for some time to come.

It was 1999, and I was having a very good year at work. An account—a high-tech robotics company that needed a lot of help—started quite small but just kept growing. This was my banner year; I was number one in sales out of 180 offices nationwide. The reward was a cruise to the Bahamas with runners-up sales reps. As if that wasn't enough, in the upcoming January (2000), I would join other top winners throughout the world in Birmingham, England. We would be presented with a trophy on this very fancy occasion. When my manager told me that I had won, I cried, not only because I was actually number one in the nation but because of the trip. My mother, now in her late eighties, suffered from dementia. With this free trip to England, I knew that the Lord was sending Terry and me to see her. We planned to take an extra week to be with her and my family.

To celebrate the win locally, I had to attend a large regional meeting in Southern California with hundreds of people in attendance. I was asked to make a speech in which I offered suggestions on how others might become number one in the country. When I got up to speak, Mary Rose, the youngest person in my office, who was seated right next to me, reminded me, "Don't forget Jesus."

I told the many eyes looking back at me how it was that I had won first place. It took hard work; it took diligence and tenacity. It took ignoring rejection and believing that this could be done. It took some sacrifice and a lot of energy, and most of all, it took trusting in Jesus, knowing that He had the best outcome for me, win or lose. I made it clear that without Jesus, we can do nothing.

> And whatever you do, do it heartily, as to the Lord and not to men, knowing that from the Lord you will receive the reward of the inheritance; for you serve the Lord Christ. (Colossians 3:23–24)

So it was in January 2000, Terry and I went to England to receive all the pomp and ceremony of a first-place winner and a first-place award. Of course, I was not so enthralled by the celebrations that were held in our (the international winners') honor. I was looking forward to going home to London to surprise my mother. My mum, though, was not so excited when she saw us. Her mind was frail. After the trial and tribulation she had borne over a lifetime, she now seemed to be giving in.

> ...In this world you will have trial and tribulation but be of good cheer for I have overcome the world. (John 16:33b)

My sister, Barbara, drove us to Brighton for a day of fresh air at the sea. My mother asked me the following day, "Carole, who was with us yesterday? Were you with us?" So sad. The disease was playing havoc with her brain. She would often look at a picture frame that held a photo of my late brother, Jimmy, and tell me, "I think Jimmy looks uncomfortable in that frame." I would always console her with the thought that Jimmy was with Jesus.

In her healthier days back in America, she once sat beside me in church, looking very peakèd. I asked her if she was all right, and she sullenly replied that she was. Later, outside the church, she told me that she had seen a vision of Jimmy, his coat thrown over his shoulder, as he would always do, standing next to Jesus. I told her that Jesus gave her that vision as confirmation that Jimmy was with Him. I had remembered how God had delivered the children of Israel out of Egypt (bondage). Would the Lord deliver Jimmy?

> That if you confess with your mouth the Lord Jesus and believe in your heart that God has raised Him from the dead, you will be saved. For with the heart one believes unto righteousness, and with the mouth confession is made unto salvation. (Romans 10:9-10)

Had Jimmy confessed the Lord Jesus and believed in his heart? My mother hungered to know that Jimmy was safe and happy. I did my best to move her heart toward trusting in Jesus for every outcome. He created Jimmy, and He knew how to handle him for the good.

> If a son asks for bread from any Father among you, will he give him a stone? ...If you then being evil know how to give good gifts to your children how much more will your heavenly Father give the Holy Spirit to those who ask Him? (Luke 11:11, 13)

Had Jimmy repented and asked Jesus for the Holy Spirit at the last moment? I had to leave that in the Hand of my Lord. I knew the truth of the gospel, so I explained more fully. My mothers debt had been paid in full. It was a free gift for all those who would receive this priceless gift. On my previous visit, I'd sat on her bed with her, giving her the truth and freedom of what Jesus had done for her; she was completely forgiven. Her small frame hunched into the corner of her single bed. She propped herself up against the wall like a timid mouse. Yet her life had proven pure meekness—meekness being strength under control. Her mind drifted back over the years of a life spent serving others and making sure that they were comfortable, never giving a thought for herself.

Let nothing be done from selfish ambition or conceit but in lowliness of mind let each esteem others better than himself. Let each of you look out not only for his own interests, but also for the interests of others. (Philippians 2:3–4)

My mother always looked out for the interests of others rather than her own. So much so that when my son Daniel was about eight years old, it seems he saw the meekness in this gentle lady and he asked if Nanny (my mum) was Jesus's wife. I laughed at the time, but, as usual, Daniel saw past the natural. Yes, Nanny was Jesus's bride, as all believers are the brides of Christ.

My mother and I talked as we always did. She did not have assurance of heaven. She was one of those humble servants who understood that she could never enter heaven by her works (as none can), but she lacked the knowledge that heaven was a free gift for those who trusted and believed in Jesus. She knew Jesus; she would always remind me after buying her few groceries that Jesus helped her carry them up the hill. She now needed assurance of eternal life.

Verily, verily I say to you, he that believes in Me has eternal life. (John 6:47)

When she was to take her final breath on this earth, she wanted the assurance that she would see Jesus, face-to-face. Oh, what glory! She said that she trusted in Jesus, and we spent time rejoicing. Now she was getting ready to leave this earth and meet her Lord and Savior.

In late April that year, I received a phone call from my brother-in-law, Doug, who said he thought I had better come to see her. He said that on Good Friday, April 21, she'd had a stroke and was now in the hospital. I flew out immediately, alone—Terry had seen her a few months earlier. God is so very good. It was on Good Friday that my brother Tony had gone to her flat to meet up with family to go to church.

Tony said our mother had not been feeling too strong, but she said to him that day, "I am coming to church."

> I was glad when they said to me, "Let us go to the house of the Lord." (Psalm 122:1)

As she said those few words, she fell backward, having had a stroke. I flew out of LAX on Saturday, and it was Easter Sunday at noon when I arrived at my mum's bedside. Her dim blue eyes were closed and there was such little life left in her, yet she acknowledged my (our) presence. The beautiful creamy skin on her face still shone. Although she could no longer speak, to communicate with us she held out her hand which was the only hand that she could now move. She would tap our hands to answer yes! I told the nurse that I had come from America and asked if it was possible to stay at the hospital with my mum, but the hospital rules would not allow it. I went home with my sister and slept in my mum's bed. We were all in shock.

I began sorting through my mum's belongings—belongings like soft water bottles that she hugged at night to keep her warm; crucifixes that I hung on her bedroom wall; the pair of glasses that she wore; a book published by the Fathers of The London Oratory of St Philip Neri.; and many photos of family. I made a display of her simple belongings, and as her children and grandchildren came, I encouraged them to take whatever they wanted as a remembrance of this godly lady. I knew that she was leaving.

On Tuesday, April 25, at 6:30 p.m., London time, our darling mother left this earth. After she had gone, my two sisters, Sandra and Barbara, sat with her. They saw her spirit leave her body.

> We are confident, yes, well pleased rather to be absent from the body and to be present with the Lord. (2 Corinthians 5:8)

This world had lost one of the Lord's humble servants, but I am sure that Jesus received her with open arms. We were all heartbroken, but I knew where she was going, which gave me much peace.

Earlier that afternoon, a priest was sent from the local parish (not her parish) to pray over my mum. I counted nineteen people around her bed. I approached him, told him her name, and asked if he would like to hear a little about who my mother was. He said that he had asked the Lord for a parking spot close to the hospital entrance so he could get there before my mum left. He said, "I believe that the Lord wants me here, as I got the best spot in the parking lot. God got me here promptly."

> But without faith it is impossible to please Him. (Hebrews 11:6)

The priest read John 14:2-3, which says,

> In My Father's house are many mansions; if it were not so, I would have told you. I go to prepare a place for you. And if I go and prepare a place for you, I will come again and receive you to Myself; that where I am, there you may be also.

I gave the priest an idea of who my mother was and told him I'd named my daughter after her. I mentioned that my family lived in Southern California.

He replied, "Oh yes, I know Southern California. I go quite often to see my friend. Then he mentioned the name of the priest who had prayed over Angela and me, sixteen years earlier.

> ...I am the First and I am the Last; Besides Me there is no God. And who proclaims as I do? (Isaiah 44:6-7a)

Jesus was right here with us. I told him about the charismatic meeting that I had attended when I was pregnant with Angela and that his friend, the priest, had prayed over Angela and me. I described how he'd touched my stomach, and how heat surged through me as if the Lord was sealing Angela. After I finished telling him, he nodded and smiled. This was no coincidence. There I was in London at King's College Hospital, where my mother was getting ready to leave this earth. The priest who was appointed (by God) to pray over my mother was a good friend of the priest who lived thousands of miles away in a different part of the world, where I happened to live. The priest in America had prayed over Angela, still in my womb, and me, sixteen years ago, and this priest in England knew him.

My God is so faithful. He knew my dear mother, and she was going to glory to meet her Lord and Savior, face-to-face.

This was the first time that my mum was going ahead of me. Normally, I was the one leaving. She would have been eighty-nine in just over four months—a life filled with humility and giving. We chose the following scripture to be read at her funeral:

> When the Son of Man comes in His glory, and all the holy angels with Him, then He will sit on the throne of His glory. All the nations will be gathered before Him, and He will separate them one from another, as a shepherd divides his sheep from the goats. And He will set the sheep on His right hand but the goats on His left. Then the King will say to those on His right hand, 'Come, you blessed of My Father, inherit the kingdom prepared for you from the foundation of the world: for I was hungry, and you gave Me food; I was thirsty and you gave me drink; I was a stranger and you took Me in; I was naked, and you clothed Me; I was sick and you visited Me; I was in prison and you came to Me.' (Matthew 25:31–36)

Before my mum passed, my nephew, Steven, and I were in the chapel at the hospital and noticed that Matthew 25:31–36 had been highlighted in the Bible that was lying there. Although the scripture speaks of nations, it seemed appropriate to read when speaking of my mother's life. I will meet her again in glory, and until then, I must continue to fulfill what the Lord has called me to.

12

Chapter

CALLED

A YEAR TO THE month later, April 2001, the large commissions I had been earning were beginning to dry up. The Lord was doing something; He was calling me out, calling me to go with Him. I always wanted to work for myself. I wondered if the Lord was asking me to open an employment office. I had a restlessness in my spirit that felt as though I was going take a step of faith.

This feeling brought a certain amount of anxiety. I sensed that I had a big challenge ahead of me, and for days and weeks, I waited for a breakthrough on what the Lord was doing. I knew that the Holy Spirit was calling me to come pray with the people. I thought, *I cannot be like the children of Israel who failed to cross the swollen River Jordan because of unbelief. I must follow my Lord. But will I put my toe in the river, believing that the waters will part? Was I to cross the Jordan?*

> You shall command the priests who bear the ark of the covenant, saying, 'When you have come to the edge of the water of the Jordan, you shall stand in the Jordan.' (Joshua 3:8)

...and as those who bore the ark came to the Jordan, and
the feet of the priests who bore the ark dipped in the
edge of the water (for the Jordan overflows all its banks
during the whole time of harvest), that the waters which
came down from upstream stood still, and rose in a heap
very far away ... (Joshua 3:15-16a)

I didn't know what the Lord had in mind, so I asked Him daily.
I had come to love working in sales and knew sales was the lifeblood
of any company. My thinking was, *Lord, if You want me to be in the
employment industry, I will continue to sell and believe that You will
provide help for the rest.* There were many obstacles in this industry.
Rates from insurance companies had skyrocketed. I had to consider that
when I put one person to work, that individual had to supply me with
a legal social security number and identification. The person must be
trustworthy and reliable, a good choice for the position, and covered by
workers compensation. The latter I would have to pay for. The list went
on—there was so much to consider; so much at stake. If I looked at it
from a natural eye, it was absolutely daunting and even unobtainable.

But He said, "The things which are impossible with
men are possible with God." (Luke 18:27)

God would have to do this because the legal aspects of putting one
person to work were staring me in the face. Everything I read about
starting a business glared at me. I knew that God's Word commanded
me to count the cost before I built.

For which of you, intending to build a tower, does not sit
down first and count the cost, whether he has enough
to finish it... (Luke 14:28)

I counted the cost and knew that I would be giving up over one
hundred thousand dollars a year to step out to nothing. How would my

family survive without my income? After all, even if it worked, I still had to start from nothing and build it up, and that could take years. *Oh Lord, I cannot do this.* I vacillated and had much agony, with anxious thoughts weighing on my heart.

> Be anxious for nothing, but in everything by prayer and supplication, with thanksgiving, let your requests be made known to God; and the peace of God, which surpasses all understanding, will guard your hearts and minds through Christ Jesus. (Philippians 4:6-7)

But wait a moment, I thought. *I am trusting in the Lord, and He will guard my heart and my mind.*

I was not trusting in myself as I knew that I would not do this if I wasn't being called to do so. Deep in my spirit, I knew that the Lord was calling me and that I would obey Him, first and foremost. In one minute, I knew that the Lord would do it all, and I would relax and breath. In the next minute, I was fearful, mainly because I still wanted my husband's blessing—and I was not getting it.

This was a huge part of the agony. I knew that, as a Christian, I was supposed to be there to help my family, not hinder them.

> Who can find a virtuous wife? For her worth is above rubies. The heart of her husband safely trusts her; So he will have no lack of gain. (Proverbs 31:10)

Would my husband and family now have a lack of gain? I cried out again to my Lord, "Please put the words that I must hear in my husband's mouth. Let these words come from You, Lord. Show me, Lord, what You would have me do." Each time that I pleaded with the Lord about this subject, I saw myself with my hands tied behind my back and my face turned toward Terry and away from the Holy Spirit's hands—silence. I continued working and trusting that the Lord would make a way.

> ...It is God who works in you both to will and do for His good pleasure. (Philippians 2:13)

About this time, a Christian friend of mine, "Sue," called me on the phone. We rarely called one another, only once or twice a year. She said that while she was praying, she'd heard the Lord say that when I "go out" with Him, I was to use the name *agape*. I put the phone down and wept profusely. You see, a day earlier I'd been working my territory and had asked, "Lord, if I go out with You, what would You have me call it?" The following Sunday at church, the pastor said that over the next three weeks, he'd be looking at the unconditional-love word, *agape*. He said he'd dissect this rich word and share three English words that described this one Greek word—sacrifice, action, and charity.

I almost screamed out loud because I knew that the Lord had confirmed His word. I nudged Terry, who had been coming to church with me quite regularly. He said, "It is just a coincidence." I knew different, and I wrote a letter to my pastor, explaining how the Lord had used him. The following week at work, I wrote the name agape on the work board in my office. Underneath it, I wrote the three words that comprised agape—sacrifice, action, charity. Yes, it would be a sacrifice, yet nothing can compare with the sacrifice that God paid for me.

> But when the fullness of the time had come, God sent forth His Son, born of a woman, born under the law, to redeem those who were under the law, that we might receive the adoption as sons. And because you are sons. God has sent forth the Spirit of His Son into your hearts, crying out, "Abba, Father!" (Galatians 4:4-6)

As for the second word, action—well, this seems to describe me. I was known as a go-getter and a doer.

But be doers of the word, and not hearer's only, deceiving yourselves. (James 1:22)

Now, I would be in action for Jesus—even better! Charity, yes, that is love. I asked the Lord to love His people through me. Only He can truly love the agape way. I asked Him for His power to surge through me with love overflowing. After the confirmation of receiving the name and my pastor defining the word, I knew that the Lord would be birthing something through me. I felt so sure of it that the following week, I spoke with my manager. I wanted to be transparent in the way the Lord would have us be. So these three—sacrifice, action, and charity—were to guide my life. I told my manager what had been taking place and that I was certain that the Lord was calling me to start my own ministry/business. I made it very clear to everyone in my office that although I would be in the employment business, mine would be more of a ministry—although I would obviously still need to sell and make money. I assured them, however, that I would sell in a completely different area from where I had been selling for them. I would do this for a year or so.

They knew me and knew that when I made a promise, I would keep it. But there was still one more thing. I still needed my husband's blessing. I cried out to Jesus, "Lord, how can I come with You when my husband has so much anguish about my giving up my salary? Lord, please put the words in his mouth."

Within a matter of days, I was in the kitchen, and Terry and his mum were sitting at the table. Terry said, "Carole, you are fifty years old now. Go ahead and start your business. If it doesn't work out, you can always get a job in sales."

My Lord had answered my plea.

So Abram departed as the LORD had spoken to him, and Lot went with him. And Abram was seventy-five years old when he departed from Haran. (Genesis 12:4)

Abram was seventy-five years old and trusted God, and that is what I would do. This was definitely the Lord's work. He had been making it clear to me that He wanted me to not go but to come! I wanted to be obedient to Him. Now came the test.

On August 28, 2001, I gave my manager one month's notice. I thought that a month would give them time to find a good replacement. Two weeks later (in the middle of my giving the company notice) America was brutally wounded by an enemy on 9/11, and the country went into a tailspin; the devastation still haunts us. We rallied in the streets with American flags and tears, and we all stood strong together. There wasn't anyone who wasn't devasted by this attack on American soil. No words can explain the pain of watching this evil act. The girls in my office said, "Carole, you cannot begin a business now; you must stay."

I said, "If it was my decision, I would probably stay, but the Holy Spirit is calling me, and I must go with Him."

Hindsight being 20/20, I now see it clearly. The Lord called me out at this difficult time so that everyone would know that He would be the one to build agape, not me.

> That they may see and know, and consider and understand together, that the hand of the LORD has done this, and the Holy One of Israel has created it. (Isaiah 41:20)

Only God could make this work now. It was my responsibility to take that large step of faith that Jesus had called me to take.

> Now faith is the substance of things hoped for, the evidence of things not seen. (Hebrews 11:1)

In my mind's eye, I could see Jesus standing before me, facing me, and smiling. He was beckoning me with His open hands, and it was as if He was saying, "One more step; keep coming." Like a toddler taking her first steps, I hesitatingly took one careful step after another. It reminded me of when Peter stepped out of the boat onto the water toward Jesus. But having taken his eyes off Jesus, he saw the fierce waves and began to sink. I wondered if I was going to sink like Peter.

> You of little faith, He said, "Why do you doubt?" (Matthew 14:31)

Why would I doubt now? The Lord had fulfilled everything that I asked from Him. He even proved His love by giving a departing gift to the ladies in my office. Before I left, I asked the Lord to please make sure the ladies in my office felt good about my leaving. I didn't know how He was going to do it, but the Lord knows our hearts. Three days before I left, I signed a one-million–dollar contract for the office. It was as if the Lord was giving them a parting gift through me. He was taking me, yet giving them something in return. I felt free to go. Some wanted to partner with me, but I had strict instructions to let the Lord begin the work.

13

Chapter

STEPPING OUT

A GAPE EMPLOYMENT WAS birthed on October 1, 2001. I kept to my promise about not selling in my old territory or speaking to any of my previous clients. I hired a young man, part-time; he spoke Spanish and helped me with the many people looking for work. Some did not have the needed paperwork, and he helped translate for me. These people came in droves, but what should I do if they were not here legally?

My memory of when I'd come into the country illegally was very fresh in my mind. I had done the same thing as these people were doing. I'm sure most of them only wanted a decent job so that they could feed their families. But how could I go against the law of the land and the law of God again?

> Let every soul be subject to the governing authorities.
> For there is no authority except from God, and the
> authorities that exist are appointed by God. Therefore
> whoever resists the authority resists the ordinance of
> God, and those who resist will bring judgement on
> themselves. (Romans 13:1–2)

I told them my own story of being in the United States illegally and that I had realized that it was wrong. I had broken God's law and the law of the land, bringing judgement on myself. Then I received Jesus and was born of the Spirit, and I felt a deep conviction to repent of my sins, and so I went back to do things according to God's law.

I knew how it felt to be looking over my shoulder and feeling guilty. I knew what It felt like to be unable to work legally. I prayed with the people and cried with them. I asked the Lord to work a miracle in their lives—His way, not mine. Today, the United States has a big problem at its borders. It is a very different and difficult situation. For those truly seeking asylum, I would like to see a compassionate immigration program. I do think, however, that we need to be very sure of who comes into the country by vetting them properly—a monumental job!

In the Old Testament, we can find instructions from God on what to do with the alien in the land—in the book of Ezekiel, for instance. For a Christian living anywhere in this world, we know that we belong to the kingdom of heaven. We currently live in our temporary home, and I am very grateful to call America my temporary home.

People from all walks of life came to Agape, desperate for work. Some had lost their high-paying jobs were devastated; they would take any job. I remembered the image of the Holy Spirit's hands at the bottom of my office door. I remembered that the Holy Spirit was calling me to pray with them. Now I knew why.

The first applicant who came looking for work was a young boy who had been born blind. I later learned that his elder brother also had been born blind. He said that the doctor had assured his parents that if they had more children, this wouldn't happen again, but it did.

I began searching for work for him with my physical eyes open, but he got himself a job with his physical eyes closed. You see others can help us if our eyes are physically blind. But what if our eyes are spiritually blind who can help us find God? I hoped I could be of some help, and I gave him an audio version of a very good book that gave a great explanation and evidence for who Jesus is. Although he was physically blind, I prayed that his eyes would be spiritually opened to receive the Savior.

> Now as Jesus passed by, He saw a man who was blind from birth. And His disciples asked Him, saying, "Rabbi, who sinned, this man or his parents, that he was born blind?" Jesus answered, "Neither this man nor his parents sinned, but that the works of God should be revealed in him." (John 9:1-3)

Jesus healed this man physically, but more importantly Jesus wanted to heal him spiritually. If you read the entire story you will find that this man had another encounter with Jesus where he realized that Jesus was the Son of God John 9:37. When his spiritual eyes were opened, then he said "Lord, I believe" And he worshipped Jesus. John 9:38 This blind man now not only saw physically, but spiritually also. He understood whom it was that had healed him physically and spiritually. Are your spiritual eyes open, allowing you to know Jesus, and He you?

While we do not look at the things which are seen, but the things which are not seen. For the things which are seen are temporary, but the things which are not seen are eternal. (2 Corinthians 4:18)

I prayed with each person who came in to the employment agency. It seemed people wanted to pray, even those who didn't believe. I would introduce Jesus to those who didn't know Him, reciting Ephesians 2:8–9. I would tell them that there is only One in whom we must trust, not only for immediate plans but for salvation. I also quoted Ephesians 2:10, explaining that they were made in the image of God for His good purpose. There were jobs with their names on them, I explained, and those jobs were from the Lord. It was His purpose for their lives. I always prayed that the Lord would open the door than no man can close. I wanted to give them hope and encouragement.

Some days I spent hours just consoling people, crying with them, loving them, and lifting them up in prayer. Some were losing their homes; some were living in their cars; some had lost their homes and cars. They needed Jesus. We helped monetarily when we were able. I wanted to fix each person's dilemma, and my heart was so very burdened.

> For God is not unjust to forget your work and labor of love which you have shown towards His name, in that you have ministered to the saints, and do minister. (Hebrews 6:10)

Was the Lord pleased with us ministering to His people? I couldn't tell if He was because each person's situation seemed so traumatic. I was hearing about lives that were desperate, and there was nothing I could do. But I could pray and believe that Jesus would work in all of their lives for good.

> And we know that all things work together for good to those who love God, to those who are called according to His purpose. (Romans 8:28)

Some days were heavy, and in those times, the Lord would send in sisters in Christ who would lift me up in prayer. It was like the roof of the building would topple, and our prayers went right to the throne of God.

> Let us therefore come boldly to the throne of grace, that we may obtain mercy and find grace to help in time of need. (Hebrews 4:16)

We obtained mercy and found grace in our time of need. Meanwhile, Terry was a little nervous about not having enough dollars to keep Agape running. He thought we should consider taking out a loan on our house and put it in the Agape account. In my heart, I knew this was not an instruction from the Lord, but it sounded secure and comfortable to me. And being weak and of the flesh, I agreed that maybe that would be a good idea. No jobs were coming in, and Agape had been in business for almost a month.

But there was that account I had been calling; they called me, asking for workers. It wasn't the ideal account. In fact, it was a high-risk account with regard to injury, so workers compensation insurance would be high. But there were other red flags. Terry and I discussed it and felt we might as well go ahead and put some people to work, seeing as nothing else was coming in. In the end, we lost twenty thousand dollars, which was part of the loan. There was no way to get it back—these guys owed millions to other big companies. I always wondered how these guys felt, as I would talk to them about Jesus continually.

A check would come in here and there for Agape, but they were always a calculating twenty thousand dollars in arrears. By the beginning of 2002, we knew it was over and what we had lost. The loss of money didn't keep me awake at night, but I am aware that we are called to be good stewards of what we have been given. Later on, on a quiet afternoon in my office, the Lord spoke to my heart. He said, *You and Terry were like Abram and Sarah with Hagar.*

> But he who was of the bondwoman was born according to the flesh, and he of the free woman through promise. (Galatians 4:23)

> Now Sarai, Abram's wife, had borne him no children. And she had an Egyptian maidservant whose name was Hagar … (Genesis 16:1)

If you read on, you will find that Abram and Sarai went ahead of God, and Hagar bore a son, Ishmael. Then God came to Sarah and Abraham and promised a son from their flesh. He was the promised son, Isaac, with whom God would establish His covenant. God had a plan, but Abraham and Sarah couldn't wait. They thought they were too old to have children and did not trust that God is all powerful (omnipotent) and can do whatever He chooses. They did it their way. This resulted in war between two peoples that has lasted until this day for Israel and many of the Arabic countries.

I saw that what I had done was just like Sarah and Abraham. Rather than wait on God, I went ahead, operating in my own flesh. I had failed to inquire of God. When I realized what I had done, I repented.

> He will be very gracious to you at the sound of your cry;
> when He hears it, He will answer you. (Isaiah 30:19b)

The Lord did answer me on the loss of the money. I was never really concerned about it because I knew that the Lord was chastening me. As Hebrews 12:6 says, "For whom the Lord loves He chastens ..." I knew that the Lord would teach me and even bring the money back another way.

Soon after, I was standing at my desk, feeling rather overwhelmed by the influx of people, many of whom were illegal. The available jobs were not as plentiful as the people. On this particular afternoon, when everything had quieted down, I heard the Lord speak. I had never heard His voice before, but it was so full of love and so gentle that it was as if Holy Spirit oil was dripping into my heart.

> My sheep hear My voice, and I know them, and they
> follow Me. (John 10:27)

And very clearly, I heard, *"Love them, encourage them, and tell them about Me. I know where these people belong, and I am dealing with them."* I stepped back from my desk with full knowledge that I had heard from my Lord. I had a clarity about my duties. It was not my place to try to fix these people; it was the Lord's. I knew my job description now, and I would do as the Lord had told me. I would love them. It would be His love through me—true love, honest love, joyful love. I would encourage them, give them hope, and tell each one about Jesus. I knew that if I was obedient to this calling that Jesus would open doors that no man can close for these people.

For a long while afterward, I would say to those looking for work what the Lord had said to me. Obviously, I could not say it in the way I'd heard it, as the voice of God could never be replicated.

> When they went, I heard the noise of their wings, like
> the noise of many waters, like the voice of the Almighty.
> (Ezekiel 1:24)

At this same time, the Lord impressed on me the two visions that He had shown me when I was a child. I responded, very unsurprised, and said, "Yes, Lord, I know." But what I didn't know was that both visions would not come to pass until Agape Employment was birthed.

> Behold, the former things have come to pass, and new
> things I declare; Before they spring forth I tell you of
> them. (Isaiah 42:9)

Shortly afterward, an acquaintance called, asking if we could provide her with some kitchen help. She was a Christian and was the director at a local college. I told her I would try. I began to pray. The Lord opened the doors for people to go to work. This college was one of several colleges, and today we still work happily with these wonderful clients. The Lords sent His people over the years, and many were hired. While the Lord was blessing His people at Agape through prayer and opening doors for work, the enemy sneaked in the back door with his lies and destruction. It has been my experience (and seems most often the case) that in a Christian's life, when the Lord does a mighty work, the enemy pursues his agenda to thwart the blessings.

14

Chapter

DECEIVED

I T WAS LATE February 2002, after Angela had turned eighteen years of age, that a decision was made that would change her life and our lives for some time. This is a story for her to tell. It has been a very long, hard road for Angela. She has been the most repentant person I have ever known. She identifies with David in the psalms. I had never seen so much agony in a person as she struggled with the circumstances at hand. But we had all failed, not just Angela. My prayer was that she would receive the freedom that comes from a repentant heart and would know the complete forgiveness of the cross.

It has taken a lot of prayer and a lot of work on her part. She has done amazingly well. It was about twelve years later that she became completely free in Jesus. Angela had touched the hem of His garment. She is in love with Jesus, who forgives all of our weaknesses. She continues to hold on to His garment, as I do.

> Now a woman, having a flow of blood for twelve years, who had spent all her livelihood on physicians and could not be healed by any, came from behind and touched the border of His garment. And immediately her flow of blood stopped. (Luke 8:43-44)

Angela understands how much Jesus loves her and that He paid the price, on the cross, in full. He has forgiven her. Scripture tells us that this woman was fearful and trembling, but she had faith and did not walk away from Jesus. Instead, Scripture says that she came to Jesus, bowed down, and told Him the whole truth. Mark 5:34 says, "And He said to her, 'Daughter, your faith has healed you, Go, in peace and be freed from your suffering." Angela went to Jesus and laid it out before Him. She told Him the truth, and she has now forgiven herself as He has forgiven her. She is now aware that she is in a position to help women who are going through what she once went through.

The year 2002 brought more very sobering news. My nephew, Nicky, my brother, Tony, and his wife's only child, was diagnosed with melanoma at the young age of thirty-two. We were all very close to Nicky. He was ten years older than my boys. When the boys were born, he came to stay with us. He picked those babies up and walked around with them like a pro. When they were two years old, he would put the garden hose down their diapers and laugh and laugh as they toddled around with diapers swelling. Nicky would take James's blankie and enjoy some quiet time. James always gave up his blankie for Nicky. Daniel had the back-up blankie.

After Angela was born, when Nicky came to visit, he would toss her up in the air and carry her on his back. No one could hug like Nicky. When he hugged you, you knew he meant it. We all loved him very much. He was like my own son. He and I talked a lot as he grew. We just got along. Nicky loved Terry too. We made many good memories. We all held out much hope for a complete healing this side of heaven for Nicky. After all, he was so young.

In 2003, he got married. He called me and told me that his baby was due in July. I told him, "She's a girl," but he insisted, "No, a boy." On July 26, 2003, Miss Lauren Kealy came into this world. This wonderful little family came to visit us the following May, when Lauren was nine months old. It wasn't hard to fall in love with her, and I did. Her first tooth came through while she was with us. Nicky loved her so much. He was a wonderful father. She was his gift.

In 2003, my son James showed up to Agape for work. I was very happy to see him. Immediately, I saw how wonderful James was with the people. He has lots of compassion for the wounded. He grew in the business very quickly. His gift of discernment and love for the people was evident. He was given a very strong sense (a supernatural gift) of who belongs where. Both Daniel and James had graduated college with a marketing degree. Daniel was doing very well and keeping very busy, running their mobile detailing business. He waited two years and then joined us at Agape. To watch them both with the same uncanny gift of discerning people and placing them in positions where they would be a good fit is extremely satisfying. They just know who belongs where. They are dynamite, working as a team.

Angela had been helping me on the administrative side since she was sixteen. She has an organized mind with the most amazing discernment. This gift is very strong in her. Up until recently, she had helped Agape in many ways; now she has her own business. With a master's degree in nutrition, the Lord placed her in a position to help women with the nutrition for their bodies and their souls.

In the natural, all of this seems quite the norm. But the Lord was working. He was answering my prayers. Terry had been watching what the Lord was doing through Agape, not only with our family but with the people who worked through Agape. Some accepted Christ, some went back to church, and some were healed in the spirit to start afresh, getting back to work and becoming useful. But I would not let them forget that the Lord had done this.

> Even from the beginning I have declared to you; Before it came to pass I proclaimed it to you, lest you should say "my idol has done this, and my carved image …" (Isaiah 48:5)

One man had a gambling addiction. His conscience had been pricked by what he saw the Lord doing in his life, and he did a U-turn—he repented. So many stories, all of them good, and all of the glory goes to Jesus. Heaven knows Agape. God was making new each one of us in our family through Agape. Jesus had His mighty hand on the pulse from the start. He has always been the president, CEO, and CFO, and the paperwork reflected that. The ultimate was when Terry gave his life to Jesus—*yes*! I would have given the world to see the joy in his mother's heart to now know that her earthly son now gives the truth of the gospel to many.

> Those who are wise shall shine like the brightness of the firmament, and those who turn many to righteousness like the stars forever and ever. (Daniel 12:3)

Terry is the rock who does all of the boring bookkeeping and keeps the boys abreast of what can and cannot be done financially. He does this for Agape to this day. Through Agape, my entire family learned the true gospel and became saved. This is success in my eyes, and it's all I ever wanted. John 4 tells us, "I have no greater Joy than to hear that my children walk in the truth." There is joy in knowing that those you love and all those who have received the truth of the gospel now walk in the truth. This gave me unspeakable joy.

> In this you greatly rejoice, though now for a little while, if need be, you have been grieved by various trials, that the genuineness of your faith, being much more precious than gold that perishes, though it is tested by fire, may be found to praise, honor, and glory at the revelation of Jesus Christ, whom having not seen you love. Though now you do not see Him, yet believing, you rejoice with joy unspeakable and full of glory, receiving the end of your faith—the salvation of your souls. (1 Peter 1:6-9)

Nicky was in fighting mode to beat this disease. I heard that the radiation made him sick. We prayed for him, but because we weren't in London, we didn't see the long struggle that ensued. Nick tried a lot of different ways to beat this demon so that he could be a father to Lauren and (Ryan born in late 2005) and a husband to his wife. There was much hope in our hearts that Nicky would survive this. When we saw him, he always looked so big and strong; he did not look ill. I've heard it said the younger the skin, the quicker this type of skin disease travels. The skin, being the largest organ of the body, carries those bad cells quickly when younger.

It was early in 2007 that Nicky called and said that he would bring the family to see us in February. He wanted to take his children to Disneyland. He said that some tumors were found on him again.

I told him, "Nick, all I have is Jesus."

He responded, "Carole, I have mocked you about Jesus, but I will take Him."

Nick arrived with his beautiful little family. We loved having them. I had a chance to talk to Nick about Jesus. He asked me to go with him to buy a Bible, and so I did. At mid-week Bible study, Nicky received Jesus. I will never forget how he, with bowed head, peeked at me from the corner of his eye. Then he imitated the way my hands were lifted and open.

> I desire therefore that men pray everywhere lifting up holy hands, without wrath and doubting ... (1 Timothy 2:8)

Nicky raised his hands, asking Jesus into his heart to be his Lord and Savior.

I was reminded of a time when Nicky was four years old. He wore a dark-brown winter coat, and I took him down the road in London to get him some sweets at the sweet shop. On our way back up the hill,

Nicky turned and looked at me, as if he was thinking about something very serious. This was the same look that he gave me at the Bible study.

When it was time for him to go back to London, I had a very hard time saying goodbye to him. I knew for sure that I would see him again, but I wasn't sure if I would see him on this side of eternity.

Just as he got ready to leave at the airport, he looked at me and said, "Carole, aren't you going to say goodbye to me, then?"

I gulped, holding back the tears and smiled, and hugged him, and Terry and I went upstairs to exit. When I looked down to the ground floor, I saw him just going through the gate. He wore a yellow T-shirt, his favorite color and mine. I wondered if this was the last time that I would see Nicky this side of eternity.

At the end of February, Nicky told me that the tumors were back, some in his head, which made him stumble. He said that those who didn't know him thought that he was drunk on a Monday morning. But my family knew that Nick had Jesus, and where Jesus is, there is freedom.

> ...and where the Spirit of the Lord is there is liberty. (2 Corinthians 3:17b)

He had life—life eternal. It was on June 1, 2007, that the Lord Jesus opened His arms and received Nicky. And Nicky was freed from the evil of the disease. We will meet again in glory!

> Merciful men are taken away, while no one considers that the righteous is taken away from evil. He shall enter into peace ... (Isaiah 57:1b–2a)

15

Chapter

COMES TO PASS

B Y 2008, AGAPE Employment wasn't only known in heaven, but it had made quite a mark on the earth too. By now, the Lord had opened the doors for many of His people to go to work. James and Daniel were doing a wonderful job. The clients and our temporary employees loved them, and they were happy helping people go to work. Angela was busy, studying and working for a physical therapist. I was still face-to-face selling and witnessing. It was around September of that year that a friend of mine (a former Muslim who had received Jesus as her Lord and Savior) asked if I would take her to a midweek all-day Christian meeting. She had no car and had no way of getting there unless I helped. I took her, not knowing that the Lord had intended for me to be there.

As I listened to the presentation, I learned that this organization (an international women's group) was active in over sixty-five countries. This organization was begun in 1938 by a woman who was called to pray in and for her neighborhood in northern California. I later read her inspiring autobiography. She was born in Ireland, and her father brought her and her sister to America to do tent evangelism. I felt so connected. This local arm now was looking for local speakers who had come to the Lord and wanted to tell how and why through their testimonies.

The testimonies would be given with the idea of giving the gospel, asking those who did not have a relationship with Jesus if they would like to receive Him. So, all those at this meeting who were interested would have to write their testimonies, following ministry guidelines and parameters.

It took a couple of months, but I did write mine. The next step was to speak it to the board of directors in order to get it approved. Mine was approved by the grace of God, and I began to speak at women's luncheons throughout Southern California. Eventually, I spoke in Colorado, Georgia, and Canada. I was now a speaker for this Christian women's group, and I had the privilege to give the truth of the gospel. But wait a minute—this sounded very familiar. Was this the second vision that I saw as a child? I was young in the vision, but when I became born again, Jesus did impress on my heart that He would bring me back to that little girl that He had created.

As I grow older, my body seems to get thinner, similar to the way I looked as a twelve-year-old. This might have been the reason that the Lord recently jogged my memory of these two visions. Although I hadn't forgotten them, I hadn't been thinking about them. Maybe He was reminding me of them because He was going to bring them to pass.

What about the vision of the woman in Africa? Would this come to pass soon too? Well, friends from my church were being called to Kenya. I had mentioned the vision of Africa to them. They were obedient to the Lord's call, and God did a mighty work through them. When they returned, they brought me a beautiful 2.5-feet-by-2-feet plaque of the continent of Africa. With much joy, I hung it in my office at Agape for all to see, especially me. Dear Purcell has since gone to glory, but Vicky, his wife, continues to bring God the glory by serving in Kenya. She tells me that she has seen an image of me in Kenya. She always asks me, "When will you come to Kenya?" I lovingly respond with, "When the Lord tells me to come."

Back in 2007 and 2008, Daniel and James married our two wonderful "daughters-in-love" (daughters-in-law). Daniel married first and chose Fallon, and Fallon chose Daniel. Fallon is a high-spirited warrior who stands for what she knows is right. She teaches her children (along with Daniel) about Jesus. James chose Jamie, and Jamie chose James. Jamie is a loving mother and wife and now a professor of English at a local college. She, along with James, considers love to be the most excellent way.

With the marriages came very special gifts from Jesus for Terry and me. On July 4, 2009, Fallon, by the hand of God, brought our first grandchild into this world. When the doctors took him from Fallon's womb, they began to sing, "He's a Yankee Doodle Dandy, Yankee Doodle ..." Sir Jude Wesley is a true American, sharing his birthday with America and always celebrating with fireworks. He is our firecracker. He is a lover of people. From the time he was born, I have always seen him as an older man, resembling his maternal grandpa. I see him with his arms around people, maybe his family, like a covering. He is sensitive and caring, with a protective spirit. What love he brings. My word for Jude in the spirit is *tabernacle*, a dwelling place.

> For a tabernacle was prepared: the first part, in which was the lampstand, the table and the showbread which is called the Sanctuary; and behind the second veil, the part of the tabernacle which is called the Holiest of All ... (Hebrews 9:2-3)

Jesus tabernacled among us.

> And thus the secrets of his heart are revealed; and so, falling down on his face, he will worship God and report that God is truly among you.
> (1 Corinthians 14:25)

Oh, but doesn't our God have a sense of humor! A few years earlier, I had become an American citizen, purely so that I would be eligible to vote. I thought it was my duty as a Christian living in America to participate in the elections. The Lord had been cultivating a Biblical worldview in me. God is still on the throne, and it is He whom I will serve. The Bible speaks clearly to me about standing by Israel, about the killing of innocent babies (in the fire)—Leviticus 18:21, Deuteronomy 12:31, Ezekiel 16:20–21, and many more.

As for the sacred union of marriage, Jesus says,

> And then He said to them "Have you not read that He who made them at the beginning made them male and female; and said, "For this reason a man shall leave his father and mother and be joined to his wife, and the two shall become one flesh? So then, they are no longer two but one flesh. Therefore what God has joined together, let not man separate." (Matthew 19:4-6)

God instituted marriage between a man and a woman for procreation. Look up these scriptures for yourself.

In late 2009, Terry retired. He had been planning a trip for us to go back to where we first met in Prince Edward Island. What a lovely thought, but I wasn't ready to go on a six-month trip. I had my dogs and my cats to consider. Jude was just a baby and wouldn't miss us yet. I prayed and prayed, and the Lord moved James and Jamie into our house. Thank the Lord for answered prayer. This trip was not to be about us, I told Terry; it must be about the Lord. We must tell those who didn't know who He is, reminding them of what He had done for them.

We left home on March 17, 2010. The Lord blessed this trip beyond expectations. We stayed in a tent two-thirds of the time and in a motel the rest. In over two hundred days, we encountered only two days of heavy rain while in our tent. We saw much of "America the Beautiful" once again. I noticed that there were fewer animals. My heart cried for the beasts of the field. I knew that the Lord created them, and we had dominion over them. I felt we could have done a better job of having dominion over them.

How long will the land mourn, and the herbs of every field wither? The beasts and birds are consumed, for the wickedness of those who dwell there … (Jeremiah 12:4)

On July 1, we went into Canada and stayed an entire month on the eastern coast. We went back to where Terry and I first met and camped in the vicinity. What a difference in Terry and me, now that Jesus had renewed us both. We now had joy.

Prince Edward Island, which we visited, is the setting for the classic children's novel *Anne of Green Gables*. We also traveled through Nova Scotia and Newfoundland. We came back into America near Franklin D. Roosevelt's home in northern Maine and continued through America, speaking with people about Jesus. We prayed on mountaintops and stopped at the beach in Fort Lauderdale to speak with a once-renowned ice skater, who was homeless and on drugs. Along with two pastors who happened to overhear our conversation, we gave the skater the truth of the gospel. She cried and gave her life to Jesus.

At Shenandoah, while hiking, we stopped to talk to a girl from Texas. She was a believer who had backslid. I gave her the gospel again. She repented and said she was ready to do a U-turn and walk back toward the Lord. The Lord brought divine appointments, and we remained faithful to tell people about Him. I have so many stories of those divine two hundred days. We were totally protected by the Lord in so many instances—every minute of every hour to do His bidding.

Meanwhile, halfway through the trip, Angela contacted us to say she was planning to get married. She had chosen Jeremy, and Jeremy had chosen Angela. They had been dating since Angela was seventeen. Jeremy was a self-starter, an entrepreneur in every sense of the word—a doer. He was a good match for Angie. They had a beautiful wedding on October 30, 2010. Some of my family came from London to celebrate the uniting of Angela and Jeremy.

I had been praying about finding a church with an evangelistic outreach. Through a friend at Agape, we found Calvary Chapel in Chino Hills. They have a group called the Call Ministry, and it was just what the Lord had ordered. Terry and I joined the Call in January 2011. There are many ways to give the gospel, and this was one of them. The Lord had me continue from where I had left off with those two provocative questions that give an idea of where a person is spiritually! When I arrived on the first Tuesday evening, it was evident that the Lord was very present.

> Have I not commanded you? Be strong and courageous;
> do not be afraid, nor be dismayed, for the LORD your
> God is with you wherever you go. (Joshua 1:9)

The Lord was going before each group as we ventured out to knock on doors and love our neighbors as ourselves.

> You shall love your neighbor as yourself. (Mark 12:31)

We continue to this day to give the love of Jesus and the truth of the gospel through the Call Ministry. I can't begin to tell you how many souls have come to the Lord through this amazing ministry. People from all walks of life have decided to receive Jesus as Lord and Savior. It can be used in whatever way the Holy Spirit desires. Each time we have taken the step of faith and go to do the Lord's bidding, He has gone before us to prepare the hearts of those He is calling.

Back at home, there was much joy in getting ready for the arrival of Jamie and James's first baby (our second grandbaby). Miss Reese was born on July 26, 2011 (the same day as Nicky's daughter, Lauren). Miss Reese is a horse-riding, airplane-flying, softball playing, lovable wild child. And I had the pleasure of looking after her from the time she was four weeks old. She would lie on my chest and sleep—that is, once I finally got her to sleep (which sometimes took an hour or so). This was a task. Once she was asleep, I sat on the couch with her for hours without moving a limb. I wasn't going to wake her up after all of that work.

Reese has her own spiritual language already, as I did at her age. Oh, what sweet love we have known—Miss Reese Angela. My spiritual name for Reese is *discerner and seer.*

> Who is wise? Let them understand these things. Who is discerning? Let them know them. For the ways of the LORD are right; The righteous will walk in them. But transgressors will stumble in them. (Hosea 14:9)

In January 2012, James stood by his desk at Agape and looked at me. He asked, "Mum, which missionaries does Agape support?" By the time he finished asking me that question, I knew that I would be going to Africa soon. Although I didn't answer James fully, I told him that I was going to be one of those missionaries. It seemed that recently, the Lord had been impressing on my heart to let go of Agape and begin to hand it over to James and Daniel and Angela (if she was interested). The boys hired a sales person to take my place. Coincidentally, this man had been to Africa at least ten times. He was very adept in compiling non-profit status paperwork. He asked if I would be interested in his doing one for Terry and me. We received nonprofit status in October 2012, and Agape Mission Projects was born. Within a month or so, Terry and I were in Nigeria. *Wait a minute,* I said to myself, *am I in Africa? Is this the fulfillment of the vision that the Lord showed me when I was a little child?* I believed it was. Terry and I went with John and his wife Sally, and we stayed with Pastor F. in his compound. We attended medical outreaches, where doctors and nurses administered health care to the people in villages. We sat with young and old and prayed with them for a complete healing in Jesus's name. We gave the gospel, and we now had a structure to follow, if need be.

In Africa most of the people came forward to receive Jesus, but it was not always genuine. Some came for what they could get. Pastor F. knew who they were. The Lord had equipped Terry and me through the Call Ministry to give the truth of the gospel, and so we did. We went to churches. One was a small church—so small that we stood outside to give the gospel. It was amazing how people came to hear and watch. They stood by their cardboard homes, leaned up against walls, watched, and listened. Many came forward to accept Jesus.

The children always stole our hearts. We loved on them, and they on us. The darkness is very heavy in Nigeria, but the Light (Jesus) is very powerful. We saw demon-possessed women writhing on the ground like snakes. Some were being delivered from the grip of Satan's claws. The first night that we were there, Terry and I heard the sound of what we thought was people chanting. Terry thought it might be Muslims worshipping, and I thought it might be witch doctors. Then we heard the name of Jesus, and we later learned there was a Christian church very close to the compound. Pastor F. explained that many Christians in Nigeria worshipped through the night. The idea was to have Jesus keep the enemy under His feet, as sinners love darkness rather than light.

> The way of the wicked is like darkness; they do not know
> what makes them stumble. (Proverbs 4:19)

By the time we returned from Nigeria, Terry and I knew why the Lord had created Agape Mission Projects. We were being called to fund-raise for the children of Nigeria. He would give them a future and a hope.

> For I know the plans that I think towards you, says the
> LORD, thoughts of peace and not of evil, to give you a
> future and a hope. (Jeremiah 29:11)

Some had lost parents to AIDS and lived in the bush. Terry encountered a two-year-old girl who wandered out of the bush, alone and naked. She just stood there, and he was filled with compassion. We could do something about this. Some even fell prey to witch doctors who took the children's organs, ground them, and used them as an aphrodisiac. But God! The Lord was coming to this village to change all of this in Jesus's name.

When the Lord wants the work done, He chooses who and when to do it. Terry and I went with Pastor F. to see the land that he had been given. The land lay dormant. There was no drinking water in this village. Back in 2004, Pastor and John looked at the overgrown vegetation on the land, and they laid a "cornerstone."

> Therefore thus says the Lord GOD: "Behold, I lay in Zion a stone for a foundation. A tried stone, a precious cornerstone, a sure foundation: Whoever believes will not act hastily. (Isaiah 28:16)

They prayed, believing for Jesus to build an orphanage. When Terry and I got there in 2012, the Lord was about to open the windows of heaven through some special donors who had responded to our fund-raising efforts.

> Says the LORD of hosts, "If I will not open for you the windows of heaven and pour out for you such blessing that there will not be room enough to receive it. And I will rebuke the devourer for your sakes, so that he will not destroy the fruit of your ground, nor shall the vine fail to bear fruit for you in the field." Says the LORD of hosts; (Malachi 3:10–11)

Pastor F. commented that the land had been in a coma until this time. So in January 2013, I contacted the sixty-five or so contacts that the Lord had given me through my work life. I thought back to when I had started my job at the recruitment office and how I wondered why the Lord was having me build those wonderful relationships. Now I knew. Some were business contacts, some friends, and some family. We told them the story of the needy children in Nigeria. On May 7, 2013, we (our donors and us, collectively) sent the first donation in the amount of six thousand dollars. The Lord began to build Okueyni Orphanage. His work had begun.

Moreover the Word of the LORD came to me, saying
"The hands of Zerubbabel have laid the foundation of
this temple; His hands shall also finish it. Then you
will know that the LORD of hosts has sent Me to you."
(Zechariah 4:8-9)

Many gave, and we watched the Lord open the hearts of those who
were called to give. Some gave sporadically, and some still give on a
consistent basis. All in all, we saw God's mighty hand at work. We barely
had to ask for donations—friends, family, and even business associates
gave. On January 26, 2016, the doors of Okueyni Orphanage were
officially opened, and the children came in—for shelter; for sustenance
for their tiny, starving bodies; for clothing; for schooling; and to hear
about Jesus, the King of Kings and Lord of Lords.

It shall come to pass that before they call, I will answer;
and while they are still speaking, I will hear. (Isaiah
65:24)

Whether they'd come from Christian or Muslim backgrounds, they
learned God's Word from the Holy Bible. This work of God became
a reality to this needy Nigerian village. On our return visit in 2017, we
heard a local government official say, "This orphanage is truly of God.
This village has been blessed because nowhere in Nigeria has this
happened before."

So he answered and said to me: "This is the Word
of the LORD to Zerubbabel: 'Not by might nor by
power, but by My Spirit" say's the LORD of hosts ...
(Zechariah 4:6)

With the many dollars that were sent by donors, Pastor F. has
managed to get a water well in place. The whole village benefits from
the clean water pumped from the well. At last count, there were over

fifty orphans living in Okueyni. There are at least another 150 children who walk from the village every day to go to school there. They receive one meal a day, which consists of rice and cassava. Cassava is a large, sweet potato–like root, a staple in the area. These children are blessed.

> And the LORD will make you the head and not the tail; you shall be above only, and not beneath, if you heed the commandments of the LORD your God, which I command you today, and be careful to observe them. (Deuteronomy 28:13)

God continues to touch hearts to give to His mighty work. Two large local churches in our area have begun to give—to give shelter from the storm of the enemy, to feed the hungry. The following scripture speaks loudly in my heart; it is the Lord giving thanks to our special donors:

> Then the righteous will answer Him, saying, "Lord, when did we see You hungry, and feed You, or thirsty and give You a drink? When did we see You a stranger and take You in, or naked and clothe You? Or when did we see You sick, or in prison, and come to You? And the King will answer and say to them, "Assuredly, I say to you, inasmuch as you did it to one of the least of these My brethren, you did it to Me." (Matthew 25:37-40)

What a wonderful legacy for all who gave and continue to give to Okueyni Orphanage.

> And He has made from one blood every nation of men on all the face of the earth, and has determined their pre-appointed times and boundaries of their dwellings, so that they should seek the Lord, in the hope that they might grope for Him and find Him, though He is not

far from each one of us; for in Him we live and have our
being ... (Acts 17:26-28)

Was this the first vision that Jesus showed me when I was so young?
Am I the lady that I saw? As the Lord took me to Africa and used Terry
and me to build an orphanage, I believe it is. When the Lord professes
to do something, He brings it to pass. I will know for sure when I am
eighty-one years of age (or thereabouts) and don a safari uniform. Only
the Lord knows.

16
Chapter
BIRTH

For our family in 2012, Okueyni Orphanage wasn't the only birth we were blessed with. On February 19, (same day as Nicky's birthday), Caleb came into this world. Caleb is Jude's younger brother and Daniel and Fallon's second child—and Terry's and my third grandbaby. I call this young man our warrior! His motor skills are beyond his age level. As of this writing, he is seven years old. He does flips in the air like a pro. His daddy is teaching him how to surf. Caleb tells us he does not like money and wants to give what he has to the homeless. He prays over people while his whole family go out and lay hands on people for a complete healing in Jesus's name. Sir Caleb Nicholas—what love we share.

In the spirit, I see people coming to Caleb to talk and ask his advice. At his young age, he has so much knowledge about God's creation and victory. Therefore, my spiritual name for Caleb is *counselor*.

> Where there is no counsel, the people fall; but in the multitude of counselors there is victory. (Proverbs 11:14)

Our warrior is victorious!

Toward the end of 2013, Angela stood in our kitchen and handed me a small package. "I think you might like what's inside," she said.

Being a little slow on the uptake at times, I opened the small box and pulled out a flat, three-inch, stick-like object. I thought of a makeup brush and began to brush my face with it.

Angela, smiling, said, "Don't you know what that is?"

I got it! I cupped my head in my hands and screamed. Angela was pregnant. *Oh, my God, You are so very good to us.* Years before, the Lord had shown Angela her children. She described the exact personalities and features of them, just as her children are today.

On May 9, 2014, at 10:00 p.m., Miss Kealy came into this world, fully breech, both legs wrapped around her neck. She was Angela and Jeremy's first baby and Terry's and my fourth grandbaby. Miss Kealy is an exuberant light that was sent into this world to bring joy. She is a natural, delicately created dancer. She twists and turns, hops, and spins like a ballerina inside a jewelry box, and she shines like the jewels in it. She has rings on her fingers and bells on her toes; she will have music wherever she goes.

She keeps up with her older cousins and can do it all. While Angela worked part-time, Kealy slept on my chest, just like her cousin Reese. Oh, sweet love—Miss Kealy Grace. My spiritual name(s) for Kealy are *established*—"You will also decree a thing and it will be established for you and light will shine on your ways ..." (Job 22:28)—and *rooted*—"As you therefore have received Christ Jesus the Lord, so walk in Him, rooted and built up in Him and established in the faith, as you have been taught, abounding in it with thanksgiving" (Colossians 2:6–7). What joy!

In June 2014, Terry and I began to evangelize for a start-up church in San Dimas. We met Joe and Liz at our church and, spirit identifying with spirit, we became friends. On November 2, 2014, Joe became Pastor Joe, and Calvary New Beginnings became a reality. Pastor Joe is a Bible teacher, and the small congregation of sheep the Lord has placed here are filled to overflowing with the pure milk (and meat) of the Word of God.

As newborn babes, desire the pure milk of the word, that
you may grow thereby, if indeed you have tasted that the
Lord is gracious. (1 Peter 2:2)

The Lord is growing mature Christians. It was from Pastor Joe that I heard the phrase "the unfair exchange," which I used in this book. We finished 2014 with much thanksgiving for what the Lord continues to do. Terry and I were evangelizing and helping our children by taking care of our gorgeous grandbabies during the week—His purpose for our lives. We were truly grateful. And we were even more grateful for the arrival of a sweet girl into our growing family. On February 9, 2015, Miss Paige came into our lives—Jamie and James's second little girl and Terry's and my fifth grandbaby. A sensitive, yet bossy, sweet singer, Miss Paige loves to sing. Her favorite song is "Twinkle, Twinkle, Little Star." She sings it using her own words.

I can see her when she is old, still singing. She loves to dance and wants to be a ballerina, which suits her perfectly. She dances with her cousin, Kealy. They sing and dance together. Paige will have music wherever she goes. Oh, sweet love—Miss Paige Rae. My spiritual name for Paige is *worship*.

When the morning stars sang together. And all the sons
of God shouted for joy. (Job 38:7)

Oh, but wait a minute. Angela was complaining that she could not lose weight. Why was her tummy so swollen? Well, it was because on May 31, 2015, we rejoiced to see Sir Titus come into this world. Yes, Kealy is just a year older than her brother—Angela and Jeremy's second baby and Terry's and my sixth grandbaby. Titus has a gorgeous mop of blond hair. He's a boat-loving, Mr. "keep it in place" and "I know how to fix it" kind of guy. He loves to be loved by Mama. Love abounding, he will be a leader, one who will pastor in some sense. His great-grandma says that he will be a leader of men. I agree. Sir Titus Jeremiah—oh, what love we share. For Titus, my spiritual word is *pastor*.

Therefore take heed to yourselves, and to all the flock, among which the Holy Spirit has made you overseers to shepherd the church of God which He purchased with His own blood. (Acts 20:28)

At the end of 2015, the Lord brought a pastor into our lives who had a ministry to Muslims. Terry and I had taken a course on the Muslim culture and beliefs so that we could witness to them, giving the love of Jesus. The Lord had called us to "go tell," so Terry and I joined with Pastor George and a few others to give the truth of the gospel to our Muslim friends. Every other Friday, we stood outside a designated mosque and engaged in conversation with our Muslim friends. Over the past three years, we have had some incredible conversations about who the true Jesus is. Some Muslim women have told me that they believe in the true Jesus—the one true God, who went to the cross to pay for our sins. They believe incognito.

The burning question is, "Who is Jesus?" Muslims would argue that he was a prophet. The Holy Bible tells us that He was not merely a prophet; rather, He is God in flesh, the eternal word of God. The name Jesus means "Jehovah saves." A fitting name for the One who saved us from hell. Muslims tell us that in the surahs (chapters) of the Koran, Allah told Mohammad that if he had doubt, he should go to the people of the Book (Jews and Christians) to find the truth. So why do they call the Holy Bible corrupt? Their Koran says that Allah protects his word. Well, if Allah protects his word, then how can the Bible be corrupt? Wouldn't Allah have protected it? I pray that our Muslim friends come to know the true Jesus. Lord, may You continue to come to them in dreams and visions, and may they know that You are the way, the truth, and the Life. Jesus said, "No one comes to the Father except through Me" (John 14:6).

Upon leaving the wonders of Christmas 2015, our growing family had something very special to look forward to. On January 14, 2016, Miss Elle arrived—the youngest of three for Fallon and Daniel, and number seven for Terry and me. Elle holds her own with her two brothers. When

Elle arrived, I had the sense of *strength*. It's no wonder that *strong* came to mind; just take a look at her name. In my writings, I mentioned the singular *El*. I wrote that El is of strength, power, and might. Yes, Elle will do what she knows she is called to do. So my spiritual name for Elle is *strength*. Miss Elle Dawn—oh, what love we know.

> Then he said to them, "Go your way, eat the fat, drink the sweet, and send portions to those for whom nothing is prepared; for this day is holy to our Lord. Do not sorrow, for the Joy of the LORD is your strength." (Nehemiah 8:10)

We had a lot to celebrate in January 2016. Miss Elle came just twelve days before Okueyni Orphanage had its official ribbon-cutting ceremony. The orphans came in (officially) by the mighty hand of the Lord.

In 2017 we went back to Nigeria to see God's work in action. The beautiful children living at Okueyni Orphanage, ranging in age from two to fourteen years, have been given a future and a hope. I also saw (in the spirit) that Nigeria was going to begin to prosper. Terry's and my fondest memory was meeting Rhema (which means *utterance* or *thing spoken*) and his parents at a medical outreach. His parents were young and hopeful. Hopeful that Rhema would walk and even run and that he would speak, as his name suggests.

At four years of age, Rhema had never walked or spoken words. His body had no control over its movements. His daddy held him in his arms with an obvious protective love. Terry and I prayed over Rhema and his parents. We looked into Rhema's eyes; they were smiling. He uttered a certain worship song that he loved. I know that Jesus was smiling as He received this sweet aroma of life from His son Rhema.

> For we are to God the fragrance of Christ among those who are being saved … (2 Corinthians 2:15)

Forever in eternity, Rhema will run and leap like the gazelle. We are still praying and believing for a complete healing for Rhema on this side of eternity.

In February 2016, Terry and I had a decision to make—to put a furry friend to sleep. Our thirteen-year-old German shepherd mix had dementia. Among the four (wayward) stray dogs and nine cats that we had given a home to over the years, Jagger, in his day, was the most intelligent, athletic dog we had ever owned. Never without a ball, he would line them up in order, having them in different parts of the back garden (his domain). Terry threw the ball for him all the time, and when I was sitting with him, he would place the ball at my feet, as if asking me to throw it. I would roll it back to him, and he would catch it by putting his paw on the ball and then spinning it back in my direction, where it landed precisely at my feet.

Suddenly, he was older. After three to four months of watching him get stuck under tables, walking into walls, and, finally, dragging a back leg, we had to make the decision to say goodbye. At the end, with tears rolling down my face, I would feed him by hand; he couldn't bend down to eat. It was torture, and I begged the Lord to take him. It seemed that the Lord was showing me what many other people have had to go through. With all the many cats and dogs that we had, we never had to put an animal down. It took everything in us to say it was time.

I tell you all of this to say that on the day that Jagger went to sleep, I had a doctor's appointment that morning. Something strange was happening to my body. They checked me and gave me a slip of paper. It read, "Cannot preclude cancer." It was a very sobering time for me. Did I have this disease in my body? It took a long time to get in to see a doctor. The doctor I saw and who was to do the small procedure fell and broke his arm and was unable to do any procedures for months. By the time I was able to meet with another doctor, it was April. I was scheduled to have the procedure on May 27. For over three months, I knew nothing. Did I have this disease, or didn't I? I wavered back and forth. *But wait a minute,* I told myself. *I'm a mature Christian. I will trust Jesus with whatever He has for me, right?*

But this was not the case. *Oh Lord, help my unbelief.*

> Jesus said to him, if you can believe, all things are possible to him who believes." Immediately the father of the child cried out and said with tears, "Lord, I believe; help my unbelief!" (Mark 9:23–24)

At times I became angry with the thought that I might be truly ill. I had to go back to my Lord, minute by minute, asking Him to make it well with my soul. I had sung that song—"It Is Well with My Soul"—many times, but did I really know what it meant? Was it well with my soul if I did have that deadly disease, and my time was up on this earth? *No, Lord, I cannot say it is well with my soul. Please help me, Lord.*

Terry and I often had this conversation, in which I, in my zeal, would say, "I cannot wait to see my Lord."

Terry would say, "It isn't that easy."

He felt that people tended to exclude the thought from their minds and live above it. I realized that although I couldn't wait to be with my Lord, somehow it seemed that this just wasn't the time to go. I struggled, yet in my thoughts was Philippians 4:4—"Rejoice in the Lord always. Again I will say, rejoice!" I knew that no matter what I was dealing with, I must praise my Lord and rejoice for what He had done for me. His will was perfect. In the depths of my soul, I claimed a clean report. I saw the Holy Spirit inside my body, pushing out any enemy that tried to take hold. It had *no* place in here because this temple, my body, belonged to the Holy Spirit.

> Or do you not know that your body is the temple of the Holy Spirit who is in you, whom you have from God … (1 Corinthians 6:19)

It wasn't until one Sunday morning, in the middle of worship at Calvary in Chino Hills, that I, at the throne of God, asked Jesus, "Lord, why haven't You given me the desire to write down all that You have done in my life?" The reply from the Lord to my heart was, *Because I haven't finished with you yet!*

Turning to Terry, with tears flowing and my rejoicing, I said, "Terry, I am not ill."

Terry said, "I know!"

I thanked the Lord and rejoiced. *But one more thing, Lord,* I thought. *When the doctor gives me the good news, have him tell me two things.* I was asking the Lord to confirm His word. I saw the doctor on June 3 but not for the results, or so I thought.

While my doctor was giving advice on a different subject, he looked through my file, pulled out a sheet of white paper, and held it up. He said, "Oh, by the way, there is nothing to be concerned about here. Your procedure proved to be very short and clear; also, it was as smooth as a baby."

The Lord had confirmed His word. I looked up to the ceiling with hands raised and praised my Lord. "Thank You, Jesus." Then, of course, I thanked the doctor. When I got outside his office, I broke down crying. It had been a long, sobering road. But I wasn't crying for me. I was crying for all of those who do not get a clean report.

Eternal life begins here on earth when we are born, and it continues on, either with Jesus forever or without Him forever.

> Jesus said to her. "I am the resurrection and the life, he
> who believes in Me, though he may die, he shall live.
> And whoever lives and believes in Me shall never die.
> Do you believe this?" (John 11:25–26)

It seems each one of us holds on tightly to life here on earth. This earthly body is all we know.

So now also Christ will be magnified in my body, whether by life or by death. For to me, to live is Christ, and to die is gain. (Philippians 1:20b–21)

I believe that I am almost up-to-date with writing this testimony. I am humbled to see how Jesus has changed Terry and me for His good purpose and glory. He can do the same with you. Maybe I wasn't addicted to drugs or in prison in the natural sense, but I was in prison spiritually. Rebellion is pride, and pride is what got Satan kicked out of heaven. Pride is dangerous and comes in many disguises. It is subtle. Proverbs 16:18 says, "Pride goes before destruction and a haughty spirit before a fall!" Before I surrendered to Jesus, I often had a haughty spirit. We must ask the Lord to show us our prideful ways, and we must repent of them, lay our thoughts out in front of the Lord, and talk to Him about them.

When Terry and I allowed the Lord to rule and reign over our marriage, we found a love, a strong attraction, and the other part of ourselves in each other. Jesus said,

"But from the beginning of the creation, God made them male and female'. For this reason, a man will leave his father and mother and be united to his wife, and the two will be one flesh; so then they are no longer two, but one flesh. Therefore what God has joined together, let not man separate." (Mark 10:6–9)

Our marriages on this earth, I believe, are a trial. One day we each will be married to Jesus as the bride of Christ. As of this writing (late 2018), Terry and I have almost finished a two-month sabbatical, traveling in our car and living in our tent (most of the time), through the Midwest and the South. We came to see the changing of the leaves, yet now, almost home, we have seen very little of the change; the weather has been too warm. But we had the most wonderful fellowship with each other and with all people. We prayed with many, talked about Jesus to all, and asked Jesus for a complete healing for those who were sick.

Before I left, I had prayed for months about this trip. I was apprehensive to leave my grandbabies and animals, and my heart was heavy at times. But Jesus always knows what we need before we ask. He has given me this time to write this book/testimony, as well as spend time with Terry, traveling and hiking, which we both wallow in. The free time in God's countryside has been exhilarating. Writing this testimony has been therapeutic for me in some areas, especially reliving the deaths that occurred in my younger days. Today, I would be very different.

I have sought my Lord and read His Word and found Him. He is not far from each one of us.

> So that they should seek the Lord, in the hope that they might grope for Him and find Him, though He is not far from each one of us; for in Him we live and move and have our being. (Acts 17:27-28a)

17

Chapter

A Chocolate for His Birthday!

WHERE DID IT all begin? With the wooden picture on the mantel in my bedroom. I left Jesus a chocolate for His birthday. And the door in the wooden picture that I thought had to be opened by Jesus. Along the way, Jesus taught me that I had to open that door to allow Him to come in and make His home with me. Is He asking you to do the same? Is it time for you to open your heart and invite Jesus in to be your Lord and Savior?

> Behold, I stand at the door and knock. If anyone hears My voice and opens the door, I will come in to them and dine with them, and they with Me. (Revelation 3:20)

At that early stage of my life, I knew that Jesus was in my bedroom. He would rub my forehead to calm my anxious thoughts. I received two visions from Him. The first one was of a woman in Africa. I thought that it was my grandma. About fifteen years ago, I learned, via my brother, that my grandma did have dealings with Africa. But even more exciting was that the Lord took us to Africa and allowed us to be a part of so much victory in the building of Okueyni Orphanage, giving so many children a future and a hope.

The One who calls you is faithful, who will also do it.
(1 Thessalonians 5:24)

The second vision, if you remember, was my speaking to an audience of people. I did speak for the international women's group for a number of years, and I have been in front of audiences at times. I hope this book will be a vehicle to speak to many. But I believe this is only a partial fulfillment, and there are more people to speak to. Is God speaking to you about something He has told you to do in His power?

Then, a little later, my heart knew that I had something to tell someone. Throughout the years, Jesus has taught me what it is that I must do for His purpose and His glory. I am to tell someone about Him. He would give me the words to speak to them, and I would trust in Him to work through me.

You shall speak My words to them, whether they hear
or whether they refuse … (Ezekiel 2:7)

I also sensed that there would be battles in life.

You therefore must endure hardships as a good soldier
of Jesus Christ. No one engaged in warfare entangles
himself with the affairs of this life, that he may please
him who enlisted him as a soldier. (2 Timothy2-4)

I found that anyone living as salt and light in this dark world will not go too long without encountering spiritual warfare. I have experienced a lot of division. See what Jesus has to say in Luke 12:51-53. But I understand that, as 2 Corinthians 10:3–5 tells us, "For though we walk in the flesh, we do not war according to the flesh. For the weapons of our warfare are not carnal but mighty in God, bringing every thought into captivity to the obedience of Christ …"

The enemy wants to silence the message that comes from the Lord through His vessels. But those who are called to speak and tell will speak when the time is right. In any given situation, I am learning to wait and pray until the Lord puts the words on my heart to speak. He will appoint the time to speak and the time to be quiet. My life has been filled with many occasions when the Lord has revealed to me knowledge of a situation or person, like a person's name or situation. It is a word of knowledge from the Lord.

But we must stay in close contact with the Lord at all times, as He reminds us in His Word to stay aware of Satan's schemes.

> Therefore take up the whole armor of God, that you may be able to withstand in the evil day, and having done all, to stand. Stand therefore, having girded your waist with truth, having put on the breastplate of righteousness, and having shod your feet with the preparation of the gospel of peace; above all, taking the shield of faith with which you will be able to quench all the fiery darts of the wicked one. And take the helmet of salvation, and the sword of the Spirit, which is the word of God; praying always with all prayer and supplication in the Spirit... (Ephesians 6:13–18)

Is there something He is asking you to speak forth for Him? Ask Him. Ask without doubting. Expect an answer.

Then there was the time I knew that I loved being around people and wanted to make them feel welcome and loved. I love people. But Jesus taught me that my love was flimsy and not pure. Only He is pure love, and He showed me that to achieve this, I must die to self—to be emptied so that His love could fill me with His pure agape love to be poured out on His people.

> And above all things have fervent love for one another, for "love will cover a multitude of sins." (1Peter 4:8)

147

Is He speaking to you about loving your neighbor? In Luke 10:29, the lawyer asked Jesus, "Who is my neighbor?" Jesus answered with the parable of the Good Samaritan (Luke 10:25–37). Samaritans were half-breeds, not the kind of people that the Jews hung around with, and vice versa. Is there someone in your life who does not fit into your idea of a neighbor or a friend, yet the Lord is asking you to love them for Him? I know He tells me this.

Then there were those special people in my life, the ones who died. Jesus taught me how to leave all of that to Him and to trust in Him alone. He is my all in all.

> I am the Alpha and the Omega, the Beginning and the
> End, the First and the Last. (Revelation 22:13)

Have you been hanging on to those loved ones who have died? There is nothing that you can do. Let them go. The Lord is perfect in all His ways. He knows how to deal with each soul. He created them.

The worst of all was when I was in total rebellion. I did it all my way. I was seeking an identity but looking in all the wrong places. My arrogant attitude pushed and prodded at any authority that stood in my way. I came into the country illegally and stepped more and more onto the enemy's turf. I dabbled with astrology and told fortunes, dragging the gifts that the Lord had given me into the devil's den—spiritual prostitution.

> For rebellion is as the sin of witchcraft, and stubbornness
> is as iniquity and idolatry. (1 Samuel 15:23)

Oh Lord, how I repented of these idols that took the place of You. Then You came to me, forgave me, and began to allow those gifts that I had wasted to be reborn—to love, to encourage, to prophesy.

Maybe you have been playing with fire. Is the Lord talking to you about idols in your life? An idol can be a simple thing. What fills your thoughts most of the day? This is your idol.

Last but not least, there has been my life, married to Terry. I chose to marry Terry, and Terry chose to marry me. We did it our way and stumbled through the desert for some years until we allowed Jesus to begin to work in us both, which He continues to do to this day. Oh, what a difference to love the person you are married to. Only Jesus puts the oasis in the desert. We must repent, unlike the Israelites who wandered in the desert for forty years (it could have taken them eleven days), and because the first generation did not repent, they did not go over to the Promised Land. Today, Terry and I have repented and now have a marriage grounded in the Promised Land of the Word of God. We have been married for forty years as of Thanksgiving Day 2018.

We all have a story to tell, whether we have known the Lord since we can remember or whether we met Him later in life. We all have a testimony of how the Lord justified us and is sanctifying us.

My prayer for those of you who do know Jesus (and He knows you) is that this book will encourage you to allow the Holy Spirit to use you the way He chooses to do. Sometimes we have our own ideas of what we want to accomplish or do with our lives. The Lord may have a different idea and purpose for your life. Remember you have been bought at a price—an astronomical price, the blood of Jesus Christ. So let the Lord lead you. He created you and knows what you need before you ask. (Matthew 6:8)

His ways are perfect. Ask Him to show you His purpose for your life. Know His Word and speak it.

> Your words were found, and I ate them, and Your word was to me the joy and rejoicing of my heart: For I am called by Your name, O LORD God of hosts. (Jeremiah 15:16)

For those of you who think you know Jesus but have realized that you only know *of* Him, my prayer for you is that you seek His face. Matthew 7:7 tells us, "For everyone who asks receives, and he who seeks finds ..." Surrender your entire life (your being) to Him. Ask Him to show you your transgressions, and repent, fully turning away from your sins. Ask Jesus to change your heart and mind, so that your desire will be for Him before all other things.

> And do not be conformed to this world, but be transformed by the renewing of your mind ... (Romans 12:2)

Ask Him to show you His desire for your life and how you can please Him so that you will know the love and the peace of having a personal relationship with the King of Kings.

> That Christ may dwell in your hearts through faith; that you, being rooted and grounded in love, may be able to comprehend with all the saints what is the width and the length and the depth and height—to know the love of Christ which passes knowledge; that you may be filled with all the fullness of God. (Ephesians 3:17–19)

For those who are doubting and disbelieving, I would pray that you have an encounter with the living God, the Lord Jesus Himself, so that He will show you who He is. He still speaks to those who are willing to hear Him and believe.

> And Thomas answered and said to Him, "My Lord and my God!" Jesus said to him, "Thomas, because you have seen Me, you have believed. Blessed are those who have not seen and yet have believed." (John 20:28:29)

Study for yourself the main events of Jesus' life. His Baptism and temptation, His Miracles, Transfiguration, Crucifixion, Resurrection and Ascension. Look at the evidence and then decide. Ask yourself, "Why and how did His disciples die?" They did not recant their faith in Christ. Would they die for a lie?

You may be seeking. You don't know much about Jesus, but you might like to know. For you, I pray that you will begin to read His Word. I pray that the Word will wash over your heart and mind while the Holy Spirit reveals the real Jesus to you. Ask Jesus to confirm His Word in you. Join a Bible-believing church and a Bible study group. Read the evidence, and allow it to prove to you that He is the eternal God, the Creator of the universe, the one who took your sin on that cross at Calvary because He loves you. All of this is so that you may come to know Him, and begin a relationship with Him. He will use you for His glory.

But know one thing: when the Lord uses you for His glory, you will experience trial and tribulation, like Jesus said. But He finished this teaching with, "But be of good cheer, I have overcome the world" (John 16:33). When your good intentions are misrepresented by the lies of the enemy, some may even say that you are doing evil rather than good. You may be defamed as an evildoer.

> But even if you should suffer for righteousness sake, you are blessed. And do not be afraid of their threats, nor be troubled. But sanctify the Lord God in your hearts, and always be ready to give a defense to everyone who asks you a reason for the hope that is in you, with meekness and fear; having a good conscience, that when they defame you as evildoers, those who revile your good conduct in Christ may be ashamed ... (1 Peter 3:14-16)

We, followers of Christ, are victorious because our Savior, Jesus, was victorious at the cross. He conquered death. This same Jesus will come back for His church.

Is it time for you to come back?

Remember followers of Christ are the church, and, collectively, the church is the bride of Christ.

The apostle Paul encourages all believers to be ready for when the Lord returns when he say's:

But I do not want you to be ignorant, brethren, concerning those who have fallen asleep, lest you sorrow as others who have no hope. For if we believe that Jesus died and rose again, even so God will bring with Him those who sleep in Jesus. (1 Thessalonians 4:13-14).

Those who die believing in Christ will rise again.

Will you be among them? Will you be watching like Jesus tells us in Luke 12:35-47

Paul encourages Christians with his message to us regarding our final victory.

Now this I say, brethren, that flesh and blood cannot inherit the kingdom of God; nor does corruption inherit incorruption. Behold I tell you a mystery: We shall not all sleep, but we shall all be changed – in a moment, in the twinkling of an eye, at the last trumpet. For the trumpet will sound, and the dead will be raised incorruptible, and we shall be changed. For this corruptible must put on incorruption, and this mortal must put on immortality. So when this corruptible has put on incorruption, and this mortal has put on immortality, then shall be brought to pass the saying that is written: "Death is swallowed up in Victory."

O Death, where is your sting?

O Hades, where is your victory?"

The sting of death is sin, and the strength of sin is the law. But thanks be to God, who gives us the victory through our Lord Jesus Christ. Therefore, my beloved brethren, be steadfast, immovable, always abounding in the work of the Lord, knowing that your labor is not in vain in the Lord. (1 Corinthians (15:50-58).

The trumpet of deliverance will sound to herald the end of the church era, when all believers will be removed from the earth at the rapture.

Does the thought of Jesus' return excite you?

I often think of His return, and wonder if I might say, "Oh! Lord, finally we are together face to face."

And then I might say "Lord, is that a piece of chocolate in Your hand?"

Printed in the United States
By Bookmasters